Antifascism Against Machismo

Antifascism Against Machismo

Tammy Kovich

with commentary by
Butch Lee and Veronica L.

Introduction by El Jones

KER
SPL
EBE
DEB
2023

Anti-Fascism Against Machismo:
Gender, Politics, and the Struggle Against Fascism
by Tammy Kovich, with commentary by Butch Lee and Veronica L.
Introduction by El Jones

Cover art by Zola

ISBN 978-1-989701-23-2
Published in 2023 by Kersplebedeb

To order copies of the book:

Kersplebedeb
CP 63560, CCCP Van Horne
Montreal, Quebec
Canada
H3W 3H8

info@kersplebedeb.com
www.kersplebedeb.com
www.leftwingbooks.net

Contents

Introduction

El Jones, February 13, 2023

PART ONE

Some snapshots:

My mummy, born in Trinidad, tells the same story every Emancipation Day (August 1). It is a story passed down from one of her great aunts, whom I believe heard it from her mother. After the abolition of slavery, my ancestor as a young girl of 4 or 5 was dancing in the streets in jubilation, singing:

> *Emancipation Day gone past*
> *Poor ol massa gonna eat long grass*

You see, the song my great ancestor was repeating was a taunt from the formerly enslaved people, pointing out to their former masters that now there was no one to do the work for them. The liberated slaves were speaking a liberated truth: that it was not African people who were lazy, incompetent, and incapable, but the whites.

My mother tells the next bit howling with laughter, repeating the punchline over and over again. Enraged upon hearing her chanting down Babylon, the white mistress ran out of her house and began screaming, "You'll eat long grass! You'll eat long grass!" slapping the little girl around the head.

This is a story of white women's violence, and of what now, following Robin DiAngelo, is known as "white fragility": a young Black girl's dancing too intolerable to bear, so this grown white woman could

7

only resort to screams and hits. But I want to think about my mother's laughter here; how to her, the white woman's violence is inconsequential—in fact, it is part of the victory of the story. We grew up with "slave silver" on our table on special occasions, which was silver cutlery engraved with a "C" for Cumberbatch, stolen from the "big house" after our ancestors in Barbados chased their white oppressors out. These signifiers of where we had been and where we are now were an inherent part of our family celebrations, but it is a joy bounded by a satisfaction in revolutionary violence. Education and respectability were certainly pitched to us as the "way out," but underneath that was this subversive vein, this tribute to our rampaging, vengeful ancestors, who took what they could of what they were owed, by force if necessary.

I think of my mother's delight at our great-ancestor as a little girl in the same way: to induce the white woman to incoherent rage, where she could only sputter ineffectively at the mocking levied at her by a small girl, only made the story more triumphant. My ancestor's joyful, derisive dancing lives on in my mother's annual screams of laughter. This unnamed white woman is and will be mocked by generations of Black women in my family. We will laugh at her for hundreds of years. The only thing that lives on is our resistance.

Fuck that white woman and her violence. I hope Black women's laughter haunts her and her line forever.

A group of enslaved women and a man sit on the steps of the Florida Club in St. Augustine, Florida, mid-19th century. A white woman, possibly a manager or overseer, stands behind them.

In Halifax, Kjipuktuk in the Mi'kmaq language, a statue of Edward Cornwallis, genocidaire extraordinaire, stood for decades in the park beside the Westin hotel. Cornwallis, the supposed "founder" of Halifax. As Mi'kmaw historian Daniel Paul taught us, in 1749, Cornwallis passed the "scalping proclamation," offering a bounty for the scalp of any Mi'kmaq man, woman, or child.[1] Cornwallis also participated in the massacre of Scottish Jacobins after the Battle of Culloden. A true hero of genocidal British imperialism!

That hotel is the site of an annual convergence of contemporary warmongers, war criminals, and genocide afficionados—the Halifax International Security Forum, started over a decade ago by Harper-era conservative Peter McKay. And so, every year, we come to protest. One year, when John McCain was here, we were fenced in by barricades with snipers on the roof of the hotel. Every year, before the protest could begin, anti-fascists would scale the statue and cover it with a sheet. In 2009, those protesting the war conference renamed the park "Peace and Freedom Park," as documented by Tony Seed and the late community journalist Robert Devet in the *Nova Scotia Advocate*.[2]

Taking her lead from Mi'kmaq women, the peace activist Betty Peterson, then in her 90s, in a speech at the park, called on everyone "to endorse the mass petition initiated by the Mi'kmaq and their allies to deCornwallize (decolonize) Nova Scotia, to remove the name of this genocidal officer from the names of all public buildings, sites and towns in Nova Scotia. Denounce the stubborn, unjustifiable resistance of the governments to this just and principled demand!"[3]

In 2017, on so-called Canada Day, a group of Indigenous women held a ceremony at the park. As Grizzly Mama cut off her braids and laid them at the foot of the statue to protest the scalping proclamation and the ongoing genocide of Indigenous women, girls, and two-spirit people, a group of five Proud Boys marched on the event. Flying the Red Ensign flag—a symbol of the Canadian far right, which had been superseded by the Maple Leaf flag in 1965 (a time before Canada's official "multiculturalism" and residential school inquiries)—the white men claimed, "This is Canada now."

"Proud Boys" attempt to disrupt antcolonial event, July 1, 2017.

We would later find out these men were in the military. They were not removed from active duty. A 2022 report commissioned by the Minister of Defense unshockingly revealed that the Canadian military is infested with white supremacists and neo-Nazis.[4] As they have against fracking thumpers destroying the land and waters, as they have against the RCMP, the women pushed back the fascists with drums, holding feathers.

It does not surprise me that there are white supremacists in Canada's white supremacist military. It does not surprise me that one of the first times the Proud Boys came to public attention in Nova Scotia was in disrupting a ceremony by Indigenous women. It does not surprise me that they were retained in the military; the same military that had been "liberating" women and girls from the Taliban in Afghanistan in the name of women's rights. It does not surprise me that the site of the Cornwallis statue was a staging ground for white supremacists and war criminals past and present, a chain of genocide and male violence stretching through time.

In a way, the Proud Boys were the most honest of all. Unlike the good white citizens of Halifax who argued that Mi'kmaq people were erasing history and that the statue was simply a benign relic of the past, the Proud Boys understood exactly what the statue meant and what they were protecting in disrupting ceremony. They were drawn there because it was a symbol of ongoing white supremacy. And they were chased away a lot more easily than the "civil," bureaucratic process the city used to delay and deny until, with the threat of Mi'kmaq people simply bringing a bulldozer, they brought it down.

When the statue of Cornwallis was finally removed in 2018, after decades of advocacy by Mi'kmaq activists, an eagle flew overhead.

It is Canada Day, 2021, and we are conducting a solidarity protest outside federal women's prison Nova Institution in Truro, Nova Scotia. In Canada today, nearly half of all federally incarcerated women are Indigenous. Indigenous women also make up the majority of those in Maximum Security. A woman once told me she was not allowed to see an elder or sweat because her "behaviour level" rating was too low, yet of course no prisoner would ever be deprived of a Bible. Another, in a poetry workshop, wrote out a devastating list of all the family members she had lost in the last year alone. She was held in the unit "for her own safety" because she was self-harming.

On the sidewalk outside the prison, our goal is to make enough noise that the women can hear us. Thunderbird Swooping Down Woman (Darlene Gilbert) and her daughter Kira, both water defenders, begin drumming and singing. Part way through the protest, the warden comes out to us. The women promptly begin singing the Mi'kmaq Honour Song, turning to each direction in turn during each round. Normally, the song is four rounds, but as the warden stood there waiting, they sang round after round after round.

Well, the warden must have been to some cultural sensitivity seminar, because that white man stood there as we turned and turned in the rain, honouring the many more directions and the strength of the women within those walls.

It was in the old Kingston Prison for Women that the Strong Woman Song was written.

And there was running through the forest after bailing out of a pickup truck with Rebecca Moore and Suzanne Patles during the Elsipogtog resistance to fracking. I was wearing heels and carrying my purse, jumping over downed logs and whipping through branches. You can't catch us RCMP. The time the uniformed US marine band, in town for the Military Tattoo, came to practice in the square outside City Hall—there was a solidarity protest for migrants at the time, led by women like Muslim activist Masuma Khan; the marines were chanted out of the space. The protests against Confederate Flag displays in Nova Scotia, led by the godmother of the movement, Dr. Lynn Jones, a 7th-generation (and more) African Nova Scotian from The Marsh in Truro.

There was the time the local right-wing rag commissioned a cartoon of me drawn like a monkey, and, when I condemned them and pointed out their racism, followed me around and harassed me online relentlessly. My mother always told me to pick my battles, so I waited a year, until I found out the cartoonist was drawing caricatures at the local comic con.

I happened to be in a boot after breaking my ankle while running (not from the cops this time.) So I limped on down to the Convention Centre, accompanied by Mi'kmaq activist Michelle Paul, waited in line, paid my $20, and demanded that that white male cartoonist draw me like a character in the Planet of the Apes. He tried to refuse, but I pointed out to him that he was happy to draw me like a monkey when those white men were paying him, and now I was paying him, so he could look me in the face and make me a monkey again. As that man sat there, I pulled up image after image of racist caricatures on my phone, just to educate him. Michelle circled around drumming as he had no choice but to listen and, finally, to attempt to apologize.

Stopping in the intersection during the summer of George Floyd resistance, forcing the cops to abandon a cruiser which was promptly draped in banners as we held a people's assembly. Fatuma Abdi (Alyaan), six months pregnant and no citizenship, facing down Prime Minister Justin Trudeau and asking him why he was deporting her brother Abdoul, asking him if he would deport his own child.

Lynn Jones, leading a protest in a snowstorm outside the Black Cultural Centre in Cherry Brook when that same Prime Minister came to offer an apology to Black youth who had been racially profiled during a trip to parliament. "We cannot let him come to our community and not defend Black lives," Lynn urged. So while the rest of the community walked by and pretended they didn't know us on their way inside, we banded together in the cold to protest mining companies and war in Latin American and African countries, our people held in prisons across this country, and to demand reparations. And Lynn again with a big "Reparations Now" banner at another apology (this Canadian government loves their toothless apologies) to the descendents of the No. 2 Construction Battalion (a Black regiment of African Nova Scotians conscripted to dig trenches and toilets during World War I; recruited at a time when the Klan-glorifying blockbuster movie *Birth of a Nation* played to sold-out crowds across North America—that is, recruited on the threat of communities being burned down and lynchings).

These fascists, in polo shirts and police uniforms, marching on us with their imperial symbols or fresh from their diversity trainings and unconscious bias trainings, sitting in a tipi or marching in a Pride parade and then advancing the pipelines (as Trudeau does), with their smears and cartoons, with their shiny instruments, with their badges and thin blue line patches. At borders, in prisons, in our university classrooms filming us. Just asking questions. Only joking. Civility. Free speech. Public safety.

And then there's us, on overpasses and sidewalks and beside rivers and statues and woods. At their parties and town halls and staged apologies and consultations.

No pasarán.

PART TWO

In late January and February of 2022, the so-called "Trucker" or "Freedom Convoy" occupied downtown Ottawa in an ostensible protest against vaccine mandates for truckers crossing the Canada-US border. The images of this occupation may seem contradictory: on the one hand there were images captured of swastikas and confederate flags, on the other were pictures of hot tubs and bouncy castles. But, as Tammy Kovich shows us in *Antifascism Against Machismo*, these things are not contradictory at all. The bouncy castles, like the children sleeping in truck cabs or used as shields at the border, mobilized ideologies of the white family and the maternal. While these images were largely dismissed as an absurdity or clownery, a sign of unseriousness or as evidence of the funds flooding the protest, it is precisely their mundanity that signals the contours of the modern right-wing movement. The "family friendly" imagery of the protest also explicitly claimed a heritage of settler colonial occupation and entitlement: to install a bouncy castle in downtown Ottawa was also to install a multi-generational claim to the land, while also framing white nationalism as "safe," "fun," "a party," and non-threatening.

Tammy's pamphlet lays out the frame through which we can understand the ways the convoy publicly created narratives that implicitly (and often explicitly) positioned them against "threatening" Black Lives Matter, Indigenous, or environmental protestors. While in reality, South Asian truckers in Canada face racism and discrimination and make up a significant proportion of drivers, the convoy leaned on the idea of the white, male, working-class trucker who sacrifices his family time to go on the road and be the breadwinner.

In contrast to the image of working-class white male freedom portrayed by convoy propaganda, Punjabi truck driver Jaskirat Singh Sidhu—who took responsibility and accepted his (unprecedented) prison sentence after missing a stop sign and crashing into a bus in 2018, killing sixteen hockey players from the Humboldt Broncos junior team—is facing deportation by the Canadian government. Sidhu was not drunk, speeding, or texting. It was a terrible accident. And yet, while separation from his family and removal is deemed an appropriate consequence for him, white truckers came to represent for the "freedom movement" (the vast majority of whom were not truckers) the literal right to occupy the centre of the country.

Following Sidhu's tragic accident, feminist Canadian journalist Nora Loreto tweeted that the "maleness, the youthfulness, and the whiteness of the victims," contributed to their "mournability" (in Judith Bulter's framing) by the Canadian public. Loreto was not minimizing the deaths of the hockey players nor the extent of the tragedy; she was, however, truthfully pointing out that in a country where residential school denialism is given mainstream platforms such as university lectures, even as the bodies of Indigenous children are being discovered by the thousands on the grounds of former residential schools, different values are accorded white male deaths than those of Muslim worshippers gunned down in a Quebec City Mosque, or the Afghan children killed during Canada's war in Afghanistan, or the Somali children tortured and murdered by Canadian "peacekeepers" in the 90s.

For this commentary, Loreto faced thousands of death and rape threats in a campaign co-ordinated by alt-right organizers. These violent threats and degrading memes towards Loreto became, for their perpetrators, part of the solidarity with Humboldt. This reaction, of course, actually proved her point: that whiteness and maleness were implicit in how the players were memorialized, so that a "threat" to this narrative by a woman, and particularly an openly feminist journalist already despised by the right, was inevitably met by a demonstration of white male rage and violence. In the right-wing narrative, respect for the players and appropriate memorialization is accompanied by deporting Brown men on the one hand, and sexually threatening dissenting white women on the other.

Similarly, in 2020, Gabriel Wortman perpetrated what is known as the worst recorded mass shooting in Canada, in the small rural community of Portapique, Nova Scotia. (This very construction of "worst mass shooting" erases the many massacres of Indigenous people, of course.) Wortman, who had a history of both assault and of domestic violence, drove around in a mock police car that he had painted and detailed in his garage. Following the murders, Cree Scholar Robyn Bourgeois wrote in an article, "Let's call the Nova Scotia mass shooting what it is: White male terrorism":

> No one seems to be drawing attention to the most prominent link connecting Canadian mass killings: all of the accused perpetrators have been men, and most of them have been white.

> White men were responsible for or currently face charges for the mass murders at ... Mayerthorpe in 2005, Moncton in 2014, Calgary in 2014, Québec City in 2017, Toronto in 2018 (a van attack) and Fredericton in 2019. Those in Vernon, B.C., in 1996, Edmonton in 2014, and Toronto in 2018 (the shooting in the city's Greektown neighbourhood) were perpetrated by racialized men.

> Given this explicitly gendered pattern of perpetration, why don't we talk about these mass murders as male terrorism?

Bourgeois went on to point out, in refutation of Trudeau's clichéd formulation that the shooting was "senseless," that:

> In fact, violence plays a fundamental role in securing male social dominance: because patriarchal domination is predicated on unfounded claims to male supremacy, violence serves to reinforce this illegitimate claim to social supremacy by force.[5]

Other commentators pointed out that while the national newspaper the *Globe & Mail* memorialized Wortman in a headline as a "denturist" with a "passion for policing," that same newspaper ran a headline about 15-year-old murder victim Tina Fontaine from Sagkeeng First Nations proclaiming that drugs and alcohol were in her system when she was killed. Bourgeois, predictably, faced a deluge of threats, racism, and calls for her to be fired, a treatment meted out to anyone who dares to identify white male violence.

While the white male violence of the mass shooter is forbidden territory, the whiteness of the victims could be mobilized by enraged racists in Nova Scotia. I testified at the province's Mass Casualty Commission, an inquiry into the failures of the RCMP in preventing the shooting. In my comments, I argued against providing the police with more weapons as a response, pointing out that the police are happy to roll armed vehicles into Black neighbourhoods to execute warrants, but allowed a white man to drive around unimpeded for hours while he murdered people. In response to my detailing of the long histories of police profiling and brutality against Black and Indigenous people in Canada and in the province, I inevitably received hate mail. In this mail, the whiteness of the victims was centred, with the explicit framing that since the victims were white, I, a Black woman, had no right to speak.

These racist responses actually mirrored what was happening implicitly in the inquiry, which is what author Desmond Cole has called a "white crisis in policing." When police confine their corruption, ineptitude, and violence to Black and Indigenous people, Black and Indigenous people who speak about police violence are informed that we are cop-haters, lowering the morale of the force, contributing

Gabriel Wortman caught on security camera.

to crime, deserving to be killed or raped since we love criminals, that we are manufacturing racism that doesn't exist in Canada, that we are privileged to be in Canada and not the US, that we should get a job and stop grifting, etc. etc. When that same policing affects white communities, criticism of the police becomes valid, but Black and Indigenous people are now still to be excised from the public space because only white deaths matter. In a further demonstration of this, the very same right-wing tabloid that drew me like a monkey and ran frequent articles denouncing and harassing me for my advocacy against the police promptly turned around and began criticizing the police themselves, which was hailed as "great journalism" and "investigative reporting." What is demonstrated here is an implicit idea of citizenship: Black people are not entitled to comment because we do not belong, whereas white men as the true citizens, and white women as the true victims, are entitled to wounding, mourning, anger, and political discussion. In fact, even as the tabloid sold papers off their own criticisms of the RCMP, they simultaneously still ran articles denouncing me as a cop-hater for writing a report on defunding the police: to them, there was no contradiction in one day blasting the RCMP as corrupt and the next targeting a Black women for saying the very same things. Only whites need apply.

One final comment on race and the mass shooting: in its aftermath, RCMP officer Heidi Stevenson, who died confronting the shooter, was immediately memorialized as a hero. At the initial press conference, before they even named or acknowledged any other victims, Stevenson (framed as a wife and mother) was lauded by the RCMP. What becomes obvious is that her actually unnecessary death caused by police ineptitude was used as a shield by the police to cover up their incompetence. This serves to illustrate the way white women's bodies are used by the patriarchal authoritarian state in service of their narratives. Perhaps ironically, people proposed that Prince Andrew High School, named for the pedophilic member of the British royal family, be renamed for Stevenson—a neat illustration of how the state maintains symbols of power but simply reshuffles the deck. When a sex offender from a family dripping in the blood of colonized people becomes too much to take, substitute a white female police officer instead.

Let me turn now to Tammy Kovich's pamphlet to bring together the threads I have traced here. As Kovich lays out:

> Hand-in-hand with the far right's condemnation of femin-ism, comes the condemnation of immigration and a particu-lar disdain for Black and Indigenous women. Combined they represent the core dangers threatening Western Civilization and white nationhood. In a somewhat contradictory dynamic, as groups advocate "putting women in their place" they simultaneously express concern for women's safety from supposedly dangerous Black and Brown men. For example, it is common for anti-immigrant arguments to be framed in terms of the threat migrant men—who are discussed as violent and/or as rapists—pose to "their women." (46)

This formulation serves to explain why white right-wing "freedom" convoy protestors can occupy downtown Ottawa while the police and military feed them intelligence and refuse to evacuate them, while Indigenous grandmothers protecting the waters face chainsaws, snipers, dogs, arrest, caging, and surveillance. This point on white women's safety is elaborated on throughout Kovich's text, tying the rhetoric of protecting white women from "threatening" Black and Brown men to discourses on policing and public safety. This serves to explain, for example, how in response to calls for defunding and a report led by a Black woman (me), the police in my city began emphasizing funding for sexual assault officers (and hate crime units), seeking to position the police as a force that keeps white women safe—at the same time as a former officer Brian Johnson (in this case a Black man) is being sued for raping girls who were under his supervision in an anti-trafficking program. (The image of the Black pimp trafficking young white girls has long been installed in Nova Scotia and can be seen in the book *Somebody's Daughter*, by Phonse Jessome, which frames all pimps as Black men from the historic community of North Preston, all victims as white girls, and the white cops and crowns as heroes. Both Black women as trafficking victims and rapist cops simply do not exist.)

Kovich's tracing of the entanglements of fascism, racism, and misogyny that uphold state violence also makes sense of the contemporary alignment of transphobia, so-called feminists, and right-wing men. An example of this ideology can be seen in a recent ad by Égard watches. The company espouses nakedly right-wing, masculinist values, first coming to attention when they countered the Gillette ad about "toxic masculinity" with an ad advocating for what Kovich summarizes as "a culture united in the belief that white male masculinity is under attack and the status of men must be protected at all costs" (36). The company has also made ads in support of the police and against defunding following the uprising against George Floyd's death.

In a follow-up ad after the confirmation hearings for Ketanji Brown Jackson, the first Black woman judge to the Supreme Court of the United States, the ad seized upon Jackson's refusal to engage with the gotcha question "what is a woman?," a question that invites transphobic and exclusionary definitions of womanhood. The ad by Égard positions itself as championing womanhood against supposed erasure by trans activists; however, a closer reading reveals that the images of womanhood to be protected are nearly exclusively white, explicitly nurturing, and explicitly feminine. For example, the footage of athletes chosen to supposedly defend women's sports are not women like Simone Biles or Serena Williams, but rather 1960s Soviet gymnast Larisa Latynina, suggesting it is white femininity in sports that must be protected, not Black African strength and dominance (it is not unremarked that it is almost exclusively African women who have been banned from athletics following rule changes around testosterone limits intended to preserve female competition.) Noticeably absent from the ad are the usual liberal feminist images of women politicians, women astronauts, women CEOs, etc. Instead, white women are shown mothering and caregiving—despite the reality that in the United States, large numbers of women working in caregiving professions, such as end of life home care, are migrant women of colour. The politician shown in the ad is

Brown Jackson; thus, despite "Gender Critical feminists" hailing the ad as powerfully advocating for women, it becomes clear that what is actually constituted in the ad is a backlash against Black women holding any political position within liberal democracy and a mobilization of white, cis womanhood against both trans women and Black women. The subtitle to the ad, "womanhood is a birthright," is more than a dog whistle: it virtually says the quiet part out loud, mobilizing what Kovich traces as the fascist investment in white womanhood as securing the nation through motherhood. This drawing together of racism, transphobia, and white womanhood makes sense of the "anti-woke" culture wars that simultaneously condemn trans rights movements and "Critical Race Theory," seeing both non-conforming bodies and Black bodies as a threat to the integrity of the state.

After providing us with a template for understanding these contemporary iterations of fascism—the men's rights movements, incels, revived white nationalism, etc.—Kovich turns to recovering the contributions of queers, women, and Women of Colour to the fight against fascism. As she argues, anti-fascist organizing is seen as white and male itself. Reifying these histories and models of organizing exclusively is one way in which dominant ideologies remain seeded in "progressive" movements, leading to the replication of gendered violence, racism, ableism, homophobia, etc, within these spaces.

Kovich's final calls offer concrete lessons from histories of feminist anti-fascist organizing for movement building today. As abolitionist and transformative justice Black feminist praxis grows—recognizing that ending our reliance on punishment, policing, and prisons also requires us to build practices of mutual care, healing, and community—Kovich's text also engages in this work of not just combatting the state but also of creating alternative ways of living. "[Resistance] took place in both the public and the private sphere, included physical confrontation, public education, labour and community organizing, surveillance and information gathering, the building of infrastructure, and so much more" (68), Kovich reminds us—a collective vision of organizing that pushes back not only against the marginalization of women, queer people, and people of colour in movement histories but also against the culture of celebrity activism currently stoked by strategic liberal media platforming of carefully chosen spokespeople.

These reminders are more important than ever as we confront the collapse of the leadership of the Black Lives Matter movement, consumed by mansions and the draw of "get the bag" Black capitalist formations; the "realignment" of male white left and and right interests promoted by self-declared leftists on YouTube, where white male resentment of their diminished role in left movements dovetails with white right-wing male resentment of the same feminists, Black people, migrant movements, etc.; the alliance between feminist discourse on preserving womanhood and women's rights and right-wing, anti-abortion men through the construction of the "trans predator"; the liberal co-optation of the mass uprising that followed George Floyd's death, countering anti-policing, anti-state protests with "Equity" initiatives, more Black board members on corporations, and government-funded

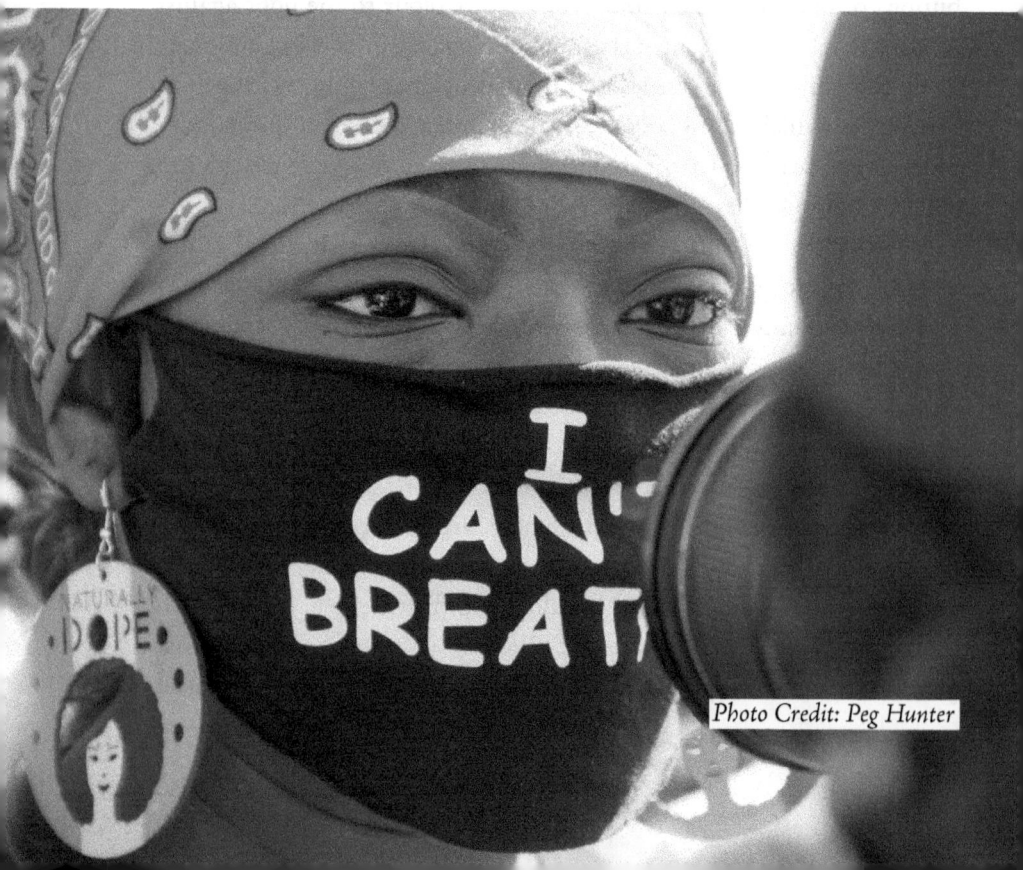

Photo Credit: Peg Hunter

entrepreneur loans (as exemplified by Black North Initiative in Canada, run by a former Bay street executive who made his career in mining and extractive industries); the ongoing expanding budgets of police; and the re-animation of fascist white "freedom" through the anti-masking, anti-vaccine movement. In these times, we are in need of principled, historically grounded, ethical, feminist organizing. Kovich provides us with a text that offers us these tools.

PART THREE

I am incredibly moved and honoured to be contributing to this book in the company of the last work of Butch Lee. When it comes to Butch Lee, those who know, know.

I first encountered Butch Lee's work when I read her book, *Jailbreak Out of History: The Re-Biography of Harriet Tubman*. That book immediately reshaped my thinking; my poem "Harriet Tubman" in my first collection of poetry *Live from the Afrikan Resistance!* is based on what she taught me. I immediately ordered all the texts I could get my hands on. I actually remember taking the bus from Winnipeg to Minneapolis reading *The Military Strategy of Women and Children* and getting pulled off the bus into a customs check: the officers were only made more suspicious by my reading choices. bell hooks, who passed in the same year as Butch, was a fan of *Night-Vision*. My friend and fellow member of our prison radio show Black Power Hour collective, historian Todd McCallum, is another fan: Todd, a historian of rebellions and uprisings, informed me of Butch Lee's comradeship in the Black liberation movement. Discovering someone else who felt her impact and knew her work felt like being in a kind of underground club. Those who know, know.

Butch Lee was calling out liberal white feminism and its violence and collusion with white supremacy clearly, cogently, and in a principled manner decades before the term "Karen" became popularized. Her indictment in *Military Strategy* of the western feminism that sees more women generals waging a war anticipated the cartoon about Hillary Clinton: "They say the next bombs will be sent by a woman"/"Really makes you feel a part of history." Lee saw how things were going, as banks now sponsor Caribana and Black History Month, as a recent corporate Black gala presented awards funded by Enbridge—the company responsible to environmental destruction, criminalization, and murder of Indigenous peoples across Turtle Island—and as #BlackExcellence and girlboss and bow down bitches are all presented as empowering and liberating.

It isn't just intellectual. Lee's work provided me with coping skills in navigating the kind of insidious gaslighting we experience as radical women. The gaslighting where we are told we need police to solve sexual assault, despite the reality that so often our rapists are cops. The gaslighting that builds new and expanded prisons with a capacity for more beds, and then situates those who resist prison expansion as not caring about the mental health needs of prisoners—as if all the suicides, self-harming, and death by toxic drugs were caused by a building and not by incarceration itself. Now we have a new prison with braille on every cell door and cells wide enough for wheelchairs, and we call that disability rights. The gaslighting that pretends cops solve hate crimes and not that they are in themselves a hate crime. The gaslighting that appoints a Somali former refugee Ahmed Hussen as Minister of Immigration and Citizenship in Canada, and then calls Black activists tools of white supremacy when we resist the deportation of other Somalis. The gaslighting that makes an Indian woman, Anita Anand, Minister of National Defense, so now she can preside over all the sexual assaults and neo-Nazis in the military. "The rich want everything, even our scars," someone once said—and now, as they frame themselves as socially just and the true victims of "woke bullying," we are ever more in need of clear analysis to get us through the fuckery. "Sprinkles on top of the pastry," Butch Lee calls it. Ha!

How do you describe how a writer you have never met has influenced and touched you? I have no personal stories to excavate, no anecdotes to tell, I only know that her words have been an incendiary device in my mind and I am grateful to her. Every year that I have encountered kersplebedeb at the Anarchist Bookfair in Halifax, I have expressed my gratitude by proxy for all that Butch Lee's work has brought. And here she is, again, in this pamphlet still going hard as fuck and not stepping off white women's necks either.

It seems so fitting that Butch Lee's last work—in her ever distinctive, urgent, prose—is a piece enthusiastically supporting radical feminist work. She ends by telling white women to step off, "to leave the dense, encumbering, blood-feeding culture of men's civilization best we can." Well, we believed in slavery that when we died, our spirits flew back to Africa, to freedom. I know Butch would want to be on that flight, and I know I carry her with me where I go.

Nazis force woman who was alleged to be in a relationship with a Jewish man to wear a sign saying "I am the hugest pig around who only does it with Jews!"(Photo: akg-images)

Anti-Fascism Against Machismo: Gender, Politics, and the Struggle Against Fascism

Tammy Kovich*

Introduction: The Rising Tide of Fascism

> It's a naturalized, state-sanctioned, normalized and deep-
> ening fascism, whose waves of violence seem to measure
> the strides of a giant... So here this question is key: What
> do we mean when we speak of feminism? Feminism cannot
> be defined at the surface level... It's a struggle that is only
> renewed by restoring the historical memory of our women
> fighters, those who have been forgotten in the dustbins of
> revolutions... We cannot think of a feminism, an anti-patri-
> archy, without anti-capitalism, without anti-fascism, with-
> out anti-racism and without class struggle...[1]

In the spring of 2017, a video of an anti-fascist being beaten at a counter demonstration in Berkeley went viral. The video depicted counter-pro-testor Louise Rosealma being punched in the face and knocked to the ground by white supremacist and founder of Identity Evropa, Nathan Damigo. On social media, in major news articles, and within move-ment circles, the video was the subject of extensive commentary. This incident and the various reactions to it tell us much about our current

---

* Originally published under the pseudonym Petronella Lee on the North Shore Counter-Info website, 2019.

moment. It reveals that we are living through a time where alt-right, white nationalist, and neo-Nazi forces are gaining momentum and becoming emboldened. As the video circulated, the response of the far right laid bare the depth of their misogyny and vividly illustrated the extent to which patriarchal ideology is a key component of their politics. Louise was doxed and viciously denigrated online—her personal information including home address and phone number was widely distributed, and her career as a sex worker was publicized. She was called disgusting and a whore, and was inundated with both rape and death threats. Photos of her being punched, as well as photos taken from her work in porn, became the backdrop for a plethora of memes appearing on both the internet and the streets. For example, on the streets of Berkeley, oversized posters appeared showing Louise's naked body beside Damigo's smiling face with the text "I'd hit that" written across.[2] Her attack and violence against women in general were promoted and celebrated. Others chimed in on the video, and their responses were equally revealing.

Far-right men rally in Charlottesville, 2017.

The reaction of liberal feminists was predictably disappointing and highlighted the many shortcomings of their political project. Some speculated about whether or not the attack would have happened under Hilary. Others framed Louise as a victim and in many cases as non-violent. Narratives circulated claiming she was attacked while attempting to de-escalate and prevent the violence of others, or was attacked unprovoked while peacefully protesting. A gendered pacifism was implied, and violence was presented as something done to Louise (as a woman), but not something that Louise (as a woman) could or would do. Hand-in-hand with these claims were calls for police involvement and the arrest of Damigo. In the style typical of carceral feminism, increased policing, criminalization, and incarceration were proposed as the appropriate response to the incident. Reactions coming from the left weren't much better, and exposed the sexism ingrained in anti-fascist politics. Posts, photos, and memes covering the incident were highly patronizing and critiqued Damigo on the basis that he was a coward for hitting a woman (assumed to be weaker and less of a threat). Despite a

antifascist witches rally

29

long history of women putting their bodies on the line to fight fascism, physical confrontation was implicitly presented as the realm of men.

Even in supposedly progressive circles, the popular image of the anti-fascist is a male body; often a white male body that borrows heavily from the aesthetics of antifa movements in Europe. Based in a tacit denial of women's agency, conversations about Louise became a matter of identity (of her being a woman), rather than a matter of politics or activity. Last and certainly not least, this incident and the fact that it got so much attention speaks to the deep-seated racism that undergirds both the left and the right. Women get attacked all the time, white supremacists beat women all of the time, and women of colour disproportionately face the brunt of it. Louise's experience went viral and garnered such broad interest undoubtedly because she is a white, conventionally attractive cis-woman.

The far right has been on the rise, and over the course of the last several years their ideas have been gaining traction. First at the level of grassroots politics, and now more and more at the level of institutional politics, far-right ideology has a notable foothold. It isn't only that far-right movements have grown, but further, that far-right ideas from the margins have seeped into the mainstream. The situation is bleak, but not hopeless. We have to know our enemy and we have a lot of work to do; however, many of the options presented to us can be found lacking. We're given the choice between a pacifying liberal feminism of "pussy hats" and "protective policing," or a reductive anti-fascism defined by machismo and sexism.

Against such a backdrop, this article seeks to examine the gendered dimensions of fascist movements and anti-fascist struggle, as well as to consider the possibilities for an anti-fascism rooted in revolutionary feminism. For the purpose of this article, I use the term fascism/fascist broadly to refer to a complicated and diverse phenomenon that includes a plethora of far-right groups, ideologies, and movements, including white nationalists, neo-Nazis, ultra-patriots, the alternative right, identitarians, and traditionalists, amongst others.[3] The article is divided into three distinct yet interrelated parts, intended to cover the politics, practices, and histories of fascism, gender, and militant resist-ance. Part 1 explores the gender politics of fascism today, Part 2 exam-ines the history of women's participation in anti-fascist resistance, and Part 3 concludes with a consideration of the challenges and prospects for developing an explicitly feminist anti-fascism.

PART 1
The Gender Politics of Fascism: Across the Spectrum of Fascist Sexisms

> Fascism, then, is an exacerbation, a more militant extension, of the patriarchal relationships between men and women that have persisted for centuries. It is a worsening of the fantasies, the violence, the misshapen desires that the whole system of gender relationships that have long pertained in European societies and those in the new world that are des-cended from them. Rather than a thing, which is categoric-ally distinct from other social and political systems, fascism is a process, which can easily recur, and wherein we can see men, and groups of men, who have commenced the journey.[4]

Following the death of Heather Heyer in Charlottesville, an organ-izer of the Unite the Right event commented that Heather was a "fat, disgusting, communist" and her death was "payback."[5] In a similar vein, comments were posted online celebrating her murder and call-ing her a "useless slut" on the grounds that "a 32-year old woman with-out children is a burden on society and has no value."[6] Beyond being attacked for her anti-fascist politics, Heather was attacked for being a woman. At the 2018 Women's March in Seattle, posters exclaiming "Make Women Property Again" made an appearance. During this same time at a similar march in Providence, members of the white nationalist group Vanguard America showed up with a banner reading "Feminists

Deserve the Rope."[7] On International Women's Day, an article on a popular neo-Nazi website proposed that an "International Burn a Witch Day" and an "International Shame a THOT Day" be celebrated as "it's only fair that we reward AND punish."[8] Only a few years earlier at an International Women's Day celebration in Sweden, neo-Nazis attacked the crowd and seriously injured five women.[9] More recently, in Santiago this past July 2018 a feminist march in support of free and legal abortion in Chile was attacked by the Social Patriotic Movement, a fascist group. Several hundred members of the group—infamous for describing feminists as animals and arguing for their sterilization—attempted to block the march and in the process covered the streets in animal blood, physically attacked the demonstrators, and stabbed three women.[10] Such examples are seemingly endless.

Incidents such as these are taking place with growing frequency, as those on the far right increasingly decry the role of feminism in propagating "Cultural Marxism" and destroying "Western Civilization."[11] Echoing the idea promoted in Nazi Germany that women's emancipation "would destroy the German race and lead to the introduction of Bolshevism," feminism (and women) are still the enemy.[12] Then as now,

patriarchy is fundamental to fascism. Taking this assertion as a starting point, this section focuses on where and how the question of gender fits into fascism. To do so, I explore the rise of the Alt-Right, examine the differing perspectives on gender and sexuality found on the contemporary far right and, finally, consider the role of the "white woman victim" trope in propping up white supremacy.

MRAS, "THE MANOSPHERE," AND THE RISE OF THE ALT-RIGHT

The current resurgence and proliferation of far-right movements in North America has frequently been linked to the rise of the Alt-Right. Short for the alternative right, the Alt-Right can be understood as a loosely organized collection of ideological tendencies, groups, podcasts, websites, think-tanks, and figureheads that have created a new breed of white supremacy. It takes inspiration from the identitarian ideas of the European New Right and is tied together by "a contempt for both liberal multiculturalism and mainstream conservatism"[13] and a "trenchant opposition to all socio-economic, cultural, and political propositions based on egalitarianism and collectivity."[14] While it is best known for its politics of white nationalism and antisemitism, politics of misogyny are also formative. Patriarchal ideology fundamentally shapes the Alt-Right, and misogyny is undoubtedly one of its central pillars.[15] The Alt-Right advocates not only for white supremacy, but more specifically for white male supremacy.[16] Sexism, rather than racism, is the gateway drug that has led many to join the Alt-Right. Romano explains: "The basic idea that 'women are getting too out of hand' is the patriarchal common denominator. And it aligns perfectly with male rage against 'social justice' activism, which in turn paves the way for white nationalism and white supremacy to gain a foothold."[17] To understand this dynamic, it is useful to look at some of the precursors to the Alt-Right movement.

Countless observers have linked the Alt-Right to the so-called "Manosphere," arguing that the Alt-Right arose in part from and continues to be closely intertwined with it.[18] Emerging in and around the 2010s, the manosphere is most simply defined as "an online antifeminist male subculture that has grown rapidly in recent years, largely outside of traditional right-wing" circles.[19] It entails a disparate network of websites, internet forums, blogs, and videos that focus on men's issues, share a chauvinistic orientation, and are united by an emphasis on male victimhood. Those involved speak out against the tyranny of SJWs (social justice warriors) and PC (politically correct) culture, and condemn feminism, along with other equity-seeking movements, as instigators of societal decline.

The manosphere first entered the public limelight in 2014 with the "Gamergate" controversy, in which a large online campaign was undertaken against a number of women who worked in the video game industry and had spoken out against sexism. Supporters of Gamergate claimed that the campaign was about defending free speech and fighting for journalistic ethics; however, in practice the campaign marked a blatant attack against women in the industry. In the words of one researcher: "This campaign took the diffuse online harassment of women and sharpened it into coordinated attacks against specific women, who faced streams of misogynistic invective, rape and death threats, and doxxing."[20] This event was a harbinger of things to come, foreshadowing the rise of the Alt-Right and offering a glimpse into the future.[21] Indeed, the tactics forged by Gamergaters, such as online harassment, targeted abuse, and doxing, were picked up by the Alt-Right and have become a common tool of the far right.[22]

The manosphere universe is comprised of a variety of different and overlapping circles, including MRAs, PUAs, MGTOWs, and INCELs. The first of which, Men's Rights Activists (MRAs) assert that the legal system, media, and society at large unfairly discriminate against men. They talk of misandry, argue that men (and not women) are oppressed and otherwise disadvantaged, and advocate on a number of different issues such as suicide, domestic abuse, and child custody.

The metaphor of "the red pill" is central; it is evoked to describe one's awakening to the dark truths of our world, such as "feminism is toxic, sexism is fake, men have it harder than women, and everything the media teaches about relationships is a lie."[23] Paul Elam, founder of the influential MRA website *A Voice for Men* has promoted beating women[24] and infamously commented "there are a lot of women who get pummeled and pumped because they are stupid (and often arrogant) enough to walk through life with the equivalent of a I'M A STUPID, CONNIVING BITCH—PLEASE RAPE ME neon sign glowing above their empty little narcissistic heads."[25] Their vitriolic hatred of women is undeniable.

Moving to the next category, Pickup Artists (PUAs) focus on helping men learn how to pick-up women and manipulate them into having sex. They talk about "the game," are obsessed with the notion of an alpha/beta male hierarchy, and advocate a predatory sexuality based on asserting dominance.[26] One of their best-known figures, Daryush Valizadeh, who writes under the name Roosh V on the PUA website *Return of Kings*, has argued for the legalization of rape on private property.[27] In May 2014, Elliot Rodger injured 14 and killed 6 at the University of California, where he hoped to "slaughter every single spoiled, stuck-up blond slut." His manifesto stated amongst other things that PUA forums had confirmed his theories "about how wicked and degenerate women really are."[28] The garbage continues and next we have Men Going Their Own Way (MGTOWs). MGTOWs are basically male separatists—they choose to avoid relationships with women altogether as a "protest against a culture destroyed by feminism."[29] Websites like *MGTOW.com* advocate men's independence from women, argue for the importance of male preservation, and discuss the fight of modern man to protect his sovereignty. Their writings are "peppered with references to a 'bitch' who will cheat, leave, use you for your money" and discussions of how "women will either trick them into raising children that aren't theirs, get pregnant intentionally in order to trap them, or falsely accuse them of rape."[30] Essentially, women are viewed as degenerate and untrustworthy sluts programmed to ruin men's lives.

Finally, Involuntary Celibates (INCELs) are a subculture of primarily young men who identify as involuntarily celibate. Influenced by
a sense of unfulfilled sexual entitlement, they speak of swallowing the
"black pill"* and conceive of their condition—defined by the absence
of romantic or sexual relationships—as immutable. They have learned
the dark truths of the world, but unlike other groups belonging to the
manosphere who set out to challenge and change that reality, incels
see their situation as fundamentally unchangeable. Their situation and
more broadly their life, is hopeless. Sparrow explains: "Incels understand biology as destiny. They regard themselves as losers in life's gen-
etic lottery. They're self-described betas, condemned by their faces and
physiques to perpetual isolation while women (whom they deride as
'Stacys') seek out the muscular, handsome males (known in the incel
lexicon as 'Chads')."[31] While some amount of blame is placed on other
men, incels primarily hold women responsible for their misery. As a
result, they denigrate women online, discuss the best ways to punish
them, and in some cases advocate mass rape, maiming, and murder.[32] In
Spring 2018, Alek Minassian drove a van into a crowd of pedestrians in
Toronto killing ten people, eight of whom were women.[33] Hours before
the attack, he made a post on Facebook celebrating the "Incel Rebellion."
In the aftermath of the incident, Jordan Peterson (psychology profes-
sor and darling of the Right) insisted that such acts of violence are
what happens when men do not have partners. To address this issue,
Peterson and his followers suggest enforced monogamy as the rational
solution to redistribute sex and prevent single men from committing
mass violence.[34]

These various online communities and the different patriarchal
orientations they represent have led many insecure, marginalized, and
otherwise struggling men to broader fascistic politics. They function
to create a culture united in the belief that white male masculinity is
under attack and the status of men must be protected at all costs. In the
context of changes in capitalism and the organization of labor, coupled

---

* Basically a more nihilistic version of the "red pill."

with various cultural-political changes said to favor women and "minorities," more and more men are embracing the far right. Reflecting on this reality, Bromma attests:

> Millions of men are losing "their" women, and "their" jobs, and it's driving them crazy... The anger of male dispossession fuels reactionary populist, fundamentalist and fascist trends in every part of the world. These right-wing movements are typically led by men of the middle classes, furious at losing the privileges they held under the previous male capitalist order. But millions of poor and de-classed men are joining in, forming a kind of united front of misogyny.[35]

In what has been referred to as the "MRA-to-white-nationalist-pipeline," men concerned with the demise of patriarchal culture and their declining material conditions in general are seduced by white supremacist thought and xenophobic ideas. As a result, they come to embrace white nationalism and advocate the vision of "an ethnically cleansed future" that is "hostile to female power."[36] Misogyny plants the seeds of fascism and operates as a stepping stone to the larger movement.

ACROSS THE SPECTRUM OF FASCIST SEXISMS

White supremacist movements have always been entangled with misogyny. As Spencer notes, their understanding of "racial hierarchy is intimately tied up with other social hierarchies."[37] That said, although virtually all fascists are anti-feminist, their views on gender and sexuality are not monolithic. In the words of one researcher: "All far rightists promote male dominance, but the kinds of male dominance they promote differ enormously."[38] There is much disagreement and frequent debate on the topic within the far right. Speaking to the place of women, some argue for the complete banishment of women from

the public sphere, while others argue that (white) women have a role to play in the white nationalist movement. On the topic of homosexuality, some argue for the extermination of all queers, while others argue for (and even celebrate) the inclusion of openly gay men. There is no consensus and substantial tensions exist. Before mapping out some of these tensions, it is useful to note the points of agreement that unite the far right in regards to the question of gender.

Despite extensive disagreement, there are a number of general ideas on which almost all agree. Some of the most common include: 1) gender essentialism; 2) gender difference; and 3) gender hierarchy. First and foremost is the idea of essentialism, understood as "the view that anything, creature, or person has an essential nature that categorically defines it, materially and/or spiritually."[39] Gender, like race, is essential—it is a biologically determined fact that defines the essence of a person and shapes everything from ability to intelligence to motivations to vices to human worth. It is a universal category that is not socially constructed but is the unchangeable product of nature.[40] Based on this understanding, the second shared idea is that of binary gender and specific gender roles. Gender is conceptualized as binary and rigid. One is born either a man or a woman, and this inescapably dictates one's place in the world. Each gender comes with a unique set of innate traits and predetermined characteristics, and as such, men are suited to specific roles and women to others.

It is worth highlighting that this position translates to agreement on opposing the notion of gender as non-binary, and thus, agreement on opposing (and frequently enacting violence against) genderqueer and trans people. In general, the far right shares a revulsion for trans people, and a particular hostility for transwomen who "are seen as men who reject their natural roles and privileges and 'voluntarily' become the hated other."[41] Lastly, the third shared idea concerns gender hierarchy and inequality. Gender is necessarily viewed as a hierarchy. It is not only that men and women are fundamentally different, but that men are fundamentally superior to women. Inequality between men and women is the product of biology and is a fact of nature—some genders, some races, some abilities, and some sexualities are simply inferior. In sum, gender is determined by nature, gender differences are immutable, and a clear gender hierarchy, where men dominate and rule, exists (and is desirable). These ideas are the basis upon which the gender ideology of the far right is built.

Drawing on these guiding threads, a number of different orientations emerge. In his study of misogyny and right-wing movements, Lyons suggests that all far-right positions on gender draw on four ideological themes—patriarchal traditionalism, demographic nationalism, male bonding through warfare, and quasi feminism. As part of this framework, patriarchal traditionalism is most frequently formulated in religious terms, promotes rigid traditional gender roles, and emphasizes the nuclear family as the mechanism for male control over women. Demographic nationalism is primarily concerned with reproduction. It is often connected to the fear that a nation or race isn't reproducing fast enough and/or that the stock is declining in quality (e.g., through racial mixing), and declares that women's main duty to the nation or race "is to have lots of babies." Male bonding through warfare is also referred to as the cult of male comradeship, and it "emphasizes warfare (hardship, risk of death, shared acts of violence and killing) as the basis for deep emotional and spiritual ties between men."[42] Historically associated with war in the trenches, it is today more commonly associated with street-fighting and militias. It sees physical confrontation as the most important aspect of life—the foundation upon which everything is built. Activities related to physicality are thus prioritized and celebrated above all others. Since women are and will always be non-combatants, they have little to no value. Lastly, quasi-feminism advocates specific rights for women, although not equality, and promotes "an expanded political role for women while accepting men's overall dominance."[43] Movements may draw heavily on a single theme or a mixture of several, and this may or may not change over time.

Along with these "warring visions of patriarchy,"[44] the approaches taken by far-right groups can be conceptualized as falling into one of two distinct categories—what I am going to refer to as patriarchal fascism and misogynistic fascism. In the category of patriarchal fascism women are considered inferior, but useful, and they have a role or particular roles to play in the white supremacist movement. This approach is exemplified by the infamous "Fourteen Words." Described as the most popular white supremacist slogan in world, "Fourteen Words" is typically written in one of two variations: "We must secure the existence of our people and a future for white children" or "Because the beauty of the White Aryan woman must not perish from the earth."[45] In both versions women are valued—as mothers, as symbols of beauty, and as protectors of the future.

This orientation has a long legacy. Throughout the 1920s, the Ku Klux Klan actively recruited women and combined white supremacy with a "specific, gendered notion of the preservation of family life and women's rights." They criticized inequality amongst whites, and promoted the "special mission of Klanswomen" to protect "pure womanhood" and the home.[46] In Germany, the Nazi Party had a women's wing—the National Socialist Women's League. According to Nazi ideology, women belonged to three areas of activity: "Kinder, Küche, Kirche" (children, kitchen, and church). Women's roles were highly restricted; however, they were also highly regarded. Mothers were seen as fighting a battle for the nation and were "accorded with the same honourable status as the soldier."[47]

Turning to our contemporary moment, this legacy continues. Coming to prominence in the 1980s, the neo-Nazi group White Aryan Resistance (WAR) created the affiliate group Aryan Women's League (AWL). It denounced the feminist movement as a Jewish conspiracy, while arguing that women had subordinate but complementary roles to play in the race war.[48] The largest neo-Nazi organization in the United States, the National Socialist Movement, has a specific

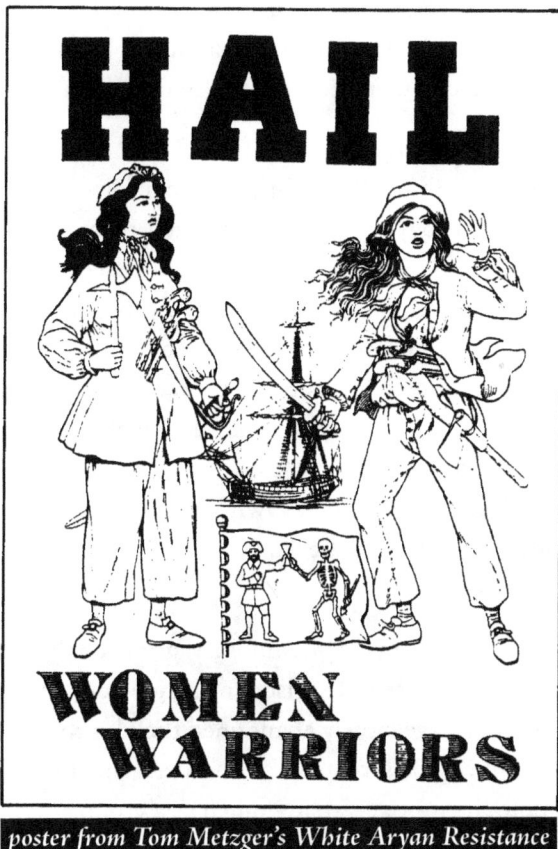

poster from Tom Metzger's White Aryan Resistance

Women's Division.[49] Another example, Women for Aryan Unity, was founded in the 1990s and has chapters on several continents. They call for the reinvention of feminism "within the parameters of Race and Revolution," and urge women to develop both domestic and survivalist skills in order to take care of home life and be ready to take up arms if their men require it.[50] Self-proclaimed western chauvinists, the Proud Boys have as one of their central tenets "venerate the housewife." They argue that "women are equal but different," interpreted to mean men go to work and women stay at home.[51] Women cannot join the Proud Boys; however, they can join the Proud Boys' Girls—a supporting group comprised of "the wives, girlfriends, and cheerleaders" of the Proud Boys.[52]

While the above examples are far from progressive, they are also far from being the worst. Over the course of the last decade, the far right's engagement with "the woman question" has taken an even darker turn. Well-known commentator on the manosphere David Futrelle elaborates:

> ...like many traditionalists, Hitler and his fellow Nazis tempered their misogyny—or at least tried to make it seem more palatable—with praise for the supposed purity and womanly honor of Aryan women who fit themselves neatly into their restricted roles. Today's neo-Nazis, or at least those who've come to Nazism through 4chan and the meme wars of the alt-right, have a much darker view of women, one influenced more by bitter misogyny of "Red Pill" pickup artists and Men Going Their Own Way than by sentimental fantasies of "Kinder, Küche, Kirche."[53]

Going beyond traditional claims about the sanctity of the family and natural gender roles, many contemporary groups influenced by the Alt-Right promote an intensely misogynistic ideology that straight-up hates women. They have largely abandoned the idea that "women have important, dignified roles to play as mothers and homemakers," to instead promote the message "that women as a group are contemptible, pathetic creatures not worthy of respect."[54] For instance, men's rights activist and white nationalist F. Roger Devlin refers to women as the new "white man's burden," arguing that traditional visions of marriage and the family "did not oppress women enough" and should be replaced with "a vision of absolute servility."[55] This is the realm of misogynistic fascism—women are not only inferior, but useless, and they have little to no role to play in the white nationalist movement. Examples of this orientation are terrifyingly ample.

Renowned white supremacist website *The Daily Stormer** has banned women from contributing to the site, virulently argues against their inclusion in anything, and has come into conflict with women associated with the older white supremacist website *Stormfront*. At several rallies in the last year, crowds of white nationalists could be found chanting "white sharia now."[56] Promoted by some on the far right, the idea of "white sharia" proposes that in a future white ethnostate "the sexuality, reproduction, daily life, and right to consent of White women should be controlled by White men."[57] In a video promoting the idea, one proponent asserts: "Under 'white sharia' our women will no longer be permitted to live their lives as sluts… And you won't have any career women invading your workplace either. Nope. Under 'white sharia' our women won't even be able to leave the home without being escorted by a male family member."[58] Many defenders of the concept also advocate making abortions forbidden for white women and mandatory for women of colour.[59] Equally vile, members of the (now-defunct) militant Atomwaffen Division encouraged the rape of white women as a tool to force the birth of more white babies,[60] and promoted the rape of non-white women as a tool to terrorize by forcing "them to carry

---

* Posts on the website argue things such as: women who have sex with Black men deserve "swift and rapid extermination" via death squads; brown men are "deranged savages" who are indefensible except in cases where they "beat the shit out of" their "bitch" girlfriends; men need the right to beat their daughters so they don't become "dumb sluts"; and "women have become complete sociopaths that collectively deserve to be punished and punished severely."

around the spawn of their master and enemy."[61] Beyond such obvious suspects, this particular orientation to women in far-right politics takes some less expected turns.

Under the umbrella of misogynist fascism, there exists a strain specifically defined by a queer misogyny. This subsection, referred to by Kirchick as "homofascism," is comprised of aggressively sexist and generally hypermasculine gay men who literally have no use for women.[62] As mentioned earlier, the far right's position on sexuality is somewhat complicated. On the one hand, LGBTQ rights are seen as a sign of social degeneration, Jewish influence, and an attack on white society. In response, it is not uncommon to see "open calls for the expulsion or violent eradication of LGBT+ people."[63] On the other hand, when speaking specifically of the "homosexual question," things are much less clear cut. Nazi Germany rounded up and slaughtered homosexuals by the tens of thousands, yet it is also common knowledge that there were gay Nazis. The most famous being Ernst Röhm, a high-ranking official and head of the Nazi Party's paramilitary force (the SA). Along with Hitler, Röhm was a "founding father of Nazism,"[64] and his particular brand of fascism "was identical to the Nazi's Party's ideology in almost all respects, save on questions of male-male eroticism." Under Röhm, homosexuality was highly regarded in the SA, where "they promoted an aggressive, hypermasculine form of homosexuality, condemning 'hysterical women of both sexes' in reference to feminine gay men." They celebrated ancient warrior cults and frequently referenced the Greek tradition of sending gay soldiers, who were believed to be the most fierce fighters, into battle.[65] In the 1980s, an explicitly gay neo-Nazi skinhead movement emerged in the UK.[66] In the late 1990s, the American Resistance Corps (ARC) was founded in North America with the goal of uniting gay and straight skinheads to create "a new era of tolerance and compassion between racist heterosexuals and homosexuals in their war against non-whites."[67]

Looking to our current period, some on the far right simply do not care about male sexuality one way or another. For instance, editor-in-chief of the influential Counter Currents Publishing Greg Johnson argues: "White Nationalism is for the interests of whites and against the interests of our racial enemies. Period. Anything else is beside the point." Similarly, the infamous alt-right figurehead Richard Spencer insists that homosexuality is a non-issue—something that has been part of European societies for millennia and isn't "something to get worked up about."[68] Against this backdrop, several openly gay figures and the ideas they promote have gained some traction on the far right. A featured writer on several alt-right websites and author of a number of books, James J. O'Meara is best known for his book *The Homo and The Negro*,[69] where he makes the argument "that gay white men represent the best of what Western culture has to offer because of their 'intelligence' and 'beauty,' and that 'Negroes' represent the worst, being incapable of achievement."[70] He insists that homosexuality is essential to Western Civilization and promotes gay participation in fascist movements.[71] O'Meara and others like him advocate a future in line with the classic Aryan fantasy of the Männerbund. Associated with male warrior tribes and homoeroticism, the concept celebrates the unique bonds between men and speaks to a social order where elite bands of men rule.[72] Male dominance is central and the fundamental building block of society isn't the church or family, but close-knit groups of organized men.

Arguably the most infamous of this camp, self-described "anarcho-fascist" Jack Donovan promotes a blend of white nationalism, gang masculinity, and androphilia (love or sex between masculine men). He calls for the establishment of a tribal order called "The Brotherhood"—an order that is comprised of men who swear an oath to each other and is based on "the way of the gang," understood as a life centered "on fighting, hierarchy, and drawing the perimeter against outsiders."[73] Utilizing violence, gangs of men are to create decentralized "homelands/autonomous zones" marked by the exclusion of women from public life.[74] Donovan is a prominent member of the neo-fascist cadre organization the Wolves of Vinland. Inspired by the theories of the late Italian philosopher Julius Evola, the group promotes a particularly anti-populist and anti-woman take on fascism. They prioritize physical fitness and combat training, and argue that the solution to western decline is "a return of heroic masculine warrior-kings."[75] All of these groups and figures advocate a politics defined by extreme hyper-masculinity based in an almost pathological veneration of "manliness" and a disdain for femininity. They reject gay culture for its association with decadence and hate effeminate men as much as they hate women.

WHITE SUPREMACY, COMPLICITY, AND THE LEGACY OF SAVIOUR POLITICS

Beyond understanding the contemporary far right's varying positions on women, it is furthermore valuable to consider the ways in which women, and white women in particular, are used as a generic symbol to promote and further white supremacy. Hand-in-hand with the far right's condemnation of feminism comes the condemnation of immigration and a particular disdain for Black and Indigenous women. Combined, these represent the core dangers threatening Western Civilization and white nationhood. In a somewhat contradictory dynamic, as groups advocate "putting women in their place," they simultaneously express concern for women's safety from supposedly dangerous Black and brown men. For example, it is common for anti-immigrant arguments to be framed in terms of the threat migrant men—who are discussed as violent and/or as rapists—pose to "their women." Founded in Finland and now with chapters across Europe and North America, the far-right vigilante group Soldiers of Odin exists for the avowed purpose of conducting street patrols to keep women safe from refugees with a propensity to rape.[76] Since taking over the White House, Donald Trump has frequently invoked the threat of "Mexico sending rapists" to justify increased border security and stricter immigration policy.[77] Such claims are not unique to discussions of migrant men alone, but pop up frequently in discussions of homegrown non-white men as well. In 2017, when white supremacist Dylann Roof opened fire and massacred nine Black churchgoers at a prayer service in Charleston, he reportedly exclaimed: "You rape our women, and you're taking over our country, and you have to go."[78] Calls to defend (white) women from the threat of the barbaric "other" play a critical role in upholding the white supremacist project.

The image of the "white woman victim" who must be protected is frequently employed by reactionary forces to whip up hysteria and justify vehemently racist actions. This classic image "implicitly calls out to white men to defend 'their women' and their nation, indeed, whiteness itself."[79] White women's bodies—understood as central to the reproduction of race and nation—become symbols to be fought for, and these symbols become powerful tools of propaganda.

Discourses of safety and appeals to patriarchal ideals of womanhood are invoked to construct the figure of the vulnerable (white) woman under attack from the dangerous (racialized) other. This dynamic functions to produce and reproduce particular race and gender formations, as well as to establish and enforce a particular vision of white nationhood. As Keskinen notes: "Gender and sexuality have not only been by-products of colonial and racial encounters, but essential for their (re)structuring."[80] The trope of the "barbaric dark-skinned rapist"—of Black and brown men as sexual predators who target white women— has been a key tool in upholding racial hierarchies and carrying out white supremacist politics. From the colonization of North America to lynchings in the United States to xenophobic attacks in Europe and much else, calls to defend women have been used to incite racialized violence and establish incredibly racist policy. A brief look into this history is telling.

The stereotype of "the Black brute" and the threat of "the Black rapist" are fundamental to the history of white supremacy in America. The idea of the Black brute was drawn on to contribute to justifications for slavery, while the myth of the Black rapist was "a political invention" cultivated to promote a "strategy of racist terror" to keep "the Negro" in check following emancipation. The myth of the Black rapist, complemented by the continued rape of Black women, helped to assure the ongoing domination and exploitation of Black people. In the aftermath of the Civil War, the claim that Black men were sexual predators was used as pretext for murder and mob violence. Lynching came to be rationalized "as a method to avenge Black men's assault's on white Southern womanhood."[81] According to Angela Davis, the myth functioned to both demonize Black men and thus legitimize contempt for them, as well as to exalt white men and excuse their brutality. She explains: "In a society where male supremacy was all-pervasive, men who were motivated by their duty to defend their women could be excused of any excesses they might commit. That their motive was sublime was able justification for the resulting barbarities." It is worth noting that as the myth gained traction, "former proponents of Black equality became increasingly afraid to associate themselves with Black people's struggle for liberation," and by the end of the nineteenth century many white women, including leading suffragists, "publicly vilified Black men for their alleged attacks on white women."[82] There is a long legacy of white women's complicity in propping up racist narratives that have very real consequences, and this is not just a matter of the distant past.

At first glance, calls for safety—things like calls for safe spaces or safe neighbourhoods—sound harmless enough. Almost everyone desires to feel safe. However, within the context of a society defined by racial domination (institutional and interpersonal racism), calls for safety often draw on and act to perpetuate racist tropes (e.g. "the Black thug," "the dangerous Black man," etc.) and frequently go hand in hand with actions and/or policies that enact racialized violence. Wang elaborates:

> When considering safety, we fail to ask the critical questions about the co-constitutive relationship between safety and violence. We need to consider the extent to which racial violence is the unspoken and necessary underside of security, particularly white security. Safety requires the removal and containment of people deemed to be threats. White civil

society has a psychic investment in the erasure and abjection of bodies that they project hostile feelings onto, which allows them peace of mind amidst the state of perpetual violence.[83]

Looking at the history of the feminist movement against sexual violence, Wang observes that calls for the safety of women were answered with the expansion of a racialized penal state. Drawing on the age-old trope of the Black male rapist, appeals to ensure women's safety acted to sanction the expansion of the police and the prison system as the state came to be presented and positioned as the protector of women (almost always conceptualized as white women).

Through the process of raising awareness about violence and fighting for aggressive prosecution of sex crimes, feminists inadvertently aided in the creation of a tough-on-crime model of policing and punishment that reflects the racism of the society from which it came; a society in which the Black male is almost always conceived of as a threat.

Similar to the function of the anti-Black myths in North American history, anti-Indigenous tropes have played an equally influential role. The convergence of racialized rape narratives and white nation-building is also integral to the history of colonization and indigenous genocide in North America. Ideas of "the savage Indian" and "Native sexual perversion" were essential to the colonial imagination.[84] These myths, combined with notions of European superiority and the righteousness of "civilizing missions," were used to justify war against Indigenous nations, the theft of Native land and resources, and the decimation of Native communities. Popular captivity narratives spread stories about the abduction and barbaric treatment of white women by violent, lust-driven Native men. These stories, along with other writings, helped to solidify the image of Native men as wanton savages and promote the idea that "both Native and white women have to be protected from Indian men."[85] In addition to providing a rationale for appropriation and assimilation, Nagel notes that stories of "Indian depredations and savagery also became a means of justifying white misbehaviour and atrocities and provided opportunities for white self-aggrandizement."[86]

More recently, the trope of "the immigrant rapist," "the barbaric refugee," and "the Muslim extremist" have been central to cries to close the borders and save the (white) nation. Examining the refugee crisis in Europe, Carroll observes that those on the right have drawn on the myth of the immigrant rapist "to call for the closing of the borders as a way to protect white, European women against the dangerous, brown men who are coming to Europe seeking asylum."[87] In addition to impacting state policy, such myths produce grassroots backlash. Last year, Italian and Polish neo-Nazi groups announced that they were joining forces to launch patrols of European beaches in order to "protect women and children from migrants" in the face of a "muslim invasion."[88] The Quebec-based Islamophobic group La Meute claimed it "was founded for the protection of our women from religious fundamentalism," and before it imploded in 2019, it repeatedly held rallies at the US-Canada border and elsewhere, protesting against "illegal refugees."[89] Calls to protect white women are used to justify everything from border policy to vigilante violence to the formation of white-nationalist paramilitary organizations.

Following a related logic, in their fight against migrants (particularly Muslims) some on the right have begun to publicly advocate for the safety of LGBTQ people. Calls to protect queers from the threat of Islamic extremists/gay-hating Muslims have been employed in an attempt to spread anti-immigrant sentiment and appeal to a different demographic. Shortly after the Pulse nightclub shooting in Orlando, white nationalist and explicit homophobe Butch Leghorn proposed taking advantage of the event. Writing on the alt-right website *The Right Stuff*, Leghorn argued: "This shooting is a very valuable wedge issue... We simply need to hammer this issue... Drive this wedge. Smash their coalition. Make it cool to be anti-Muslim because Liberalism."[90] Over the past year, "gay pride" marches that go almost exclusively through Muslim neighbourhoods have been organized by fascists in France, Sweden, and the UK.[91] Their calls to protect women, just like their calls to protect LGBTQ people, are of course disingenuous. They hate women and queers, but calls for their protection are a politically useful mechanism. Under these circumstances, Faye aptly notes that the task of feminist and queer liberation "cannot be merely sexual or gendered, but it must also be sharply critical of its alignment with whiteness as a system of persecution."[92] This is not just a matter of being aware of opportunistic white nationalists duplicitously using calls for LGTBQ safety to further their vile agenda, but also of critically evaluating the ways in which queer movements themselves buttress and reinforce white supremacy.

In regards to this responsibility, it is worth keeping in mind that the LGBTQ movement, like the feminist movement, has a history of pushing for safety in a manner that has had violent consequences for others. Examining the history of the LGBTQ movement in the United States, Hanhardt observes that appeals to safety have had racialized consequences. Since the 1970s, activist responses to anti-LGBTQ violence have taken one of two forms: the establishment of protected gay territories and the identification of anti-LGBTQ violence as a criminal category. Rooted in the implicit assumption that white gays need to be protected from violent (often read as Black) criminals, these two approaches have led to gentrification and mass incarceration—both of which disproportionally impact and devastate Black communities. Hanhardt explains:

> Messy distinctions between crime and violence, safety and justice, underscore the flexibility of concepts such as risk and their centrality to the politics of development. Here risk is simultaneously the value of speculative capital (real estate) and the justification for crime control (bad neighborhoods), the ever-present threat to gay autonomy (violence), and the symptom of irresponsibility (the designation "at risk").[93]

Calls for the creation of safe spaces came to be interpreted as calls for state violence in the form of criminalization and privatization, and through this process, became inextricably linked to spatial development and crime control strategies that play out along race and class lines.

There's a lot that needs to be challenged and much organizing to be done, and knowing the nuanced ins and outs of the forces we face is advantageous. Given that misogyny is a foundational element of contemporary far-right politics, it is valuable to know its specific role and function. This, however, is only one piece of the puzzle, and it is useful to consider other things. As we strive to challenge the rise of the fascism, it is worth looking back to the anti-fascist resistance that came before us.

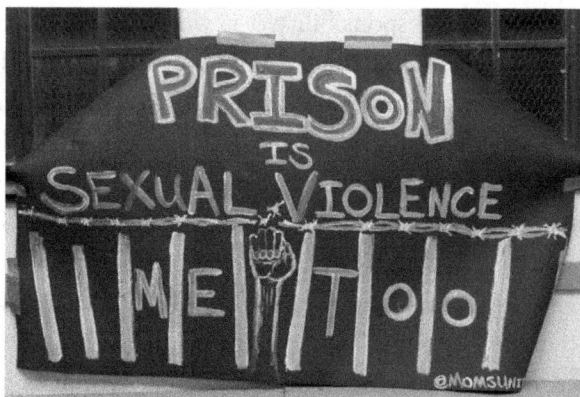

PART 2
Against Heroes: An Incomplete History of Women's Anti-Fascist Resistance

> The past does not pass; the dead are not dead, for they continue to move us today... These ghosts have not risen simply to be put to rest, but to speak in the manner for which they were killed; some of them must be battled anew in our hearts.[94]

For as long as there has been fascism, there has been anti-fascist resistance, and from its origins onwards to our present moment, women and queers have been active participants. However, these histories are routinely glossed over, and while there has been much talk of our "grandfather's anti-fascism" there is much less said about the anti-fascism of our grandmothers. Speaking to the politics of anti-fascist history, Richet notes: "Most of the sources of the history of antifascism deal with the political space occupied by men. This is the case of the fascist sources built on the assumption that women could not be autonomous political subjects. It is also the case of the sources collected by the antifascist groups whose male leadership shared similar assumptions."[95] This has an impact on anti-fascism in our present moment. When people think about or hear the term anti-fascist, the image most likely to pop into their head is not CeCe McDonald* or an armed partisan women, but a generic anti-racist skinhead dude or perhaps the anti-fascist man as depicted in classic propaganda posters with rifle, sickle, and hammer in hand. Against such trends, this section considers the gendering of history and explores women's participation in antifascist resistance during the first half of the twentieth century. The intention is not to provide an exhaustive account, but to provide a snapshot of a history too frequently forgotten and, in the process, to challenge the dominant image of the anti-fascist hero. To the extent to which such an image holds a certain pervasiveness, it acts only to hinder actions and limit possibilities.

----

* CeCe McDonald is a Black transwoman who was attacked by a Nazi in June 2011. McDonald and a group of friends were confronted by another group of people spewing racist and transphobic remarks at them. One of the women in the other group smashed a glass in McDonald's face and punched her. After a fight between the two groups broke out, the woman's ex-boyfriend assaulted McDonald, whose face was already bleeding from the glass, and threw her into the street. The man, with fists clenched, began pursuing McDonald. She quickly pulled a pair of scissors from her purse and stabbed the man in the chest as he lunged towards her. The man died. He was later found to have a swastika tattooed on his chest. She went to prison for 19 months of her 41-month sentence, despite having obviously been defending herself against a racist, transphobic Nazi who was threatening her life.

GENDER, MEMORY, AND THE STORIES WE TELL

The stories and, more importantly, the histories we tell matter—they frame events, contextualize theory, and situate agential subjects. Anti-fascism and anti-fascist history are not gender neutral, or race or class neutral for that matter. Gender plays a huge role in how we think about anti-fascism and how its history is commonly told. The history of anti-fascist struggle is depicted as the history of great moments and even greater men. It is a history of the heroic and necessarily male subjects who dared to fight back against the behemoth of fascism. If women or queers do appear in these histories, they are predominantly presented as secondary characters—as minor participants, romantic partners, or bystanders. In the realm of revolutionary history, there is a long legacy of women's activities being dismissed as: a) personal/private/home matters (e.g. bread riots; various feminist campaigns, and even the march that sparked the Russian Revolution, etc. are framed as home issues, not disciplined politics); or b) an irrational/emotional matter (e.g., they act from eruptions of emotions, and thus are inclined to spontaneity but not organized politics). Women's involvement in explicitly political movements in the public sphere, as well as the day-to-day support, reproductive, and behind-the-scenes work they perform in the private sphere, is simply disregarded.* Specific figures and activities are glorified and romanticized, while others are neglected and downplayed.

This common approach to history leads to the erasure of particular experiences, the loss of whole histories, and, beyond that, a skewed

---

* This dynamic is made worse by the fact that there is generally less documentation of women's involvement. Women were more likely to be illiterate and thus unable to write down their ideas and experiences. And even if they were literate, they were less likely to have the opportunity or time to record their thoughts. Furthermore, so much of antifascist history (at least in the period around the Second World War) was recorded by traditional political organizations and their leaderships, from which women were most often excluded.

and inaccurate picture. The creation and dissemination of accounts of radical history shape our collective political imagination and influence the events and actions thought to be desirable (and even possible). They convey specific ideas about who counts as history, what counts as history, and by default, what counts as political work and who can be a political actor. In sum, histories frequently present a hierarchy of who and what matters, and when the accounts are particularly gendered (and thus exclusionary) they stand in the way of challenging a fascist threat steeped in misogyny. As a result, it is important to look to the margins of history and seek out alternative accounts.

WOMEN AGAINST FASCISM

As already mentioned, women, femmes, and queers have been active participants in anti-fascist struggles for as long as there has been fascism. Their involvement is as diverse as it is extensive, and any attempt at a comprehensive telling is beyond the scope of this piece of writing. With this in mind, I take a narrow and inevitably limited approach to presenting anti-fascist history. While the histories of anti-fascist women and queers frequently dovetail, they are also different things and it would be impossible to cover both in this text. The vibrant legacy of queers against fascism is a history in its own right.* Thus, this section focuses exclusively on women. It draws on a small sampling of case studies from Europe, Africa, and North America to examine women's resistance to the rise of fascism following the First World War. Contrary to popular notions, women were involved in all aspects of the historical fight against fascism. Ingrid Strobl, feminist historian and former

---

* There are so many amazing stories. While outside of the scope of this article, I wanted to include at least one demonstrative example. Raad van Verzt (Resistance Council) was a group in the Dutch anti-fascist resistance. The group was founded by the gay artist Willem Arondeus and was comprised of many openly queer members, including the well-known lesbian cellist Frieda Belinfante. The group engaged in a variety of activities, but focused primarily on forging documents for the Jewish community in Amsterdam to help them escape Nazi persecution. While they had initial success with forging records, they eventually encountered a problem—the forged documents could be discovered as fakes by cross-referencing their information with the records kept in the Amsterdam Public Records Office. In response, late one evening the group burned the Public Records Office to the ground and, in the process, destroyed a key resource used by the Nazis to hunt Jews and other "degenerates." Following this sensational act, the group was hotly pursued by Nazis forces and, tragically, many of them were quickly arrested and executed. Right before his execution, Willem Arondeus passed these final words to his lawyer: "Let it be known that homosexuals are not cowards."

political prisoner associated with the women's guerrilla group Rote Zora, elaborates: "They were activists in urban brigades, the ghetto underground, and partisan units. They printed and distributed the illegal press; they forged papers; they transported weapons and themselves participated in armed actions. They organized underground movements and ghetto uprisings; they were political cadres and military commanders of groups."[96] To explore this further, it is instructive to look at resistance in Ethiopia, Spain, and Yugoslavia.

As of 1934, Ethiopia was one of just two African countries that had not been colonized by Europe.[97] Unfortunately, this was not to last, and in October of 1935 Mussolini's forces invaded Ethiopia. After capturing the capital the following year, Mussolini declared Ethiopia

Frieda Belinfante

Ethiopian woman in war clothing getting prepared for combat. 1935. Credit: Alamy Stock Photo

part of the Italian Empire, ushering in a period of fascist occupation. Resistance to the occupation, to fascism and to colonialism, commenced immediately and lasted until Italy was expelled in 1941. From the beginning, women participated in the struggle in large numbers and fulfilled many critical roles. Reflecting on this period, historian Aregawi Berhe contends that women's participation was crucial, arguing that while it is difficult to assess their military contribution, "their supplementary support activities, spying and sabotage actions in some instances were decisive." During the occupation, the Ethiopian Women's Volunteer Service Association (EWVSA) was turned into "a clandestine movement of resistance." Women who were part of the association engaged in a diversity of activities, ranging from supplying those fighting in the field with clothes, food, bandages, and ammunition, to providing shelter, forging important documents, producing propaganda, and gathering intelligence.[98] Some women became camp-followers, women who travelled to the front and took care of maintaining weapons, as well as feeding and providing medical care to those engaged in fighting.[99]

Other women fraternized with Italian soldiers and artfully engaged in deception to further the struggle. Women took Italian soldiers, including high-ranking officers, as lovers to build a false sense of trust and gain access to information and materials. With a relationship established, women took the opportunity to steal arms, and it was not uncommon for these women to kill their lovers in order to do so.[100] Such relationships were used as a tool of sabotage as well: after pretending be a defector and declaring their allegiance to fascism, women would supply their lover with false information and point the Italians in the wrong direction. Women took Italian lovers, found employment as domestic servants, or ran drinking houses to gather intelligence and collective sensitive information, such as the location of arms and ammunition depots or plans for upcoming offensives.[101]

In addition to these roles, women were also actively involved in the military aspect of the struggle. Some women became guerilla fighters and fought on the battlefield, and some even led fighters and planned military operations. Although wars in Ethiopia were predominantly fought by men, women were not entirely excluded from warfare.[102] For instance, in circumstances where a wife or daughter—in the absence of a male successor—inherited a family's land and weapons, "they were expected to perform the duties attached to the land and weapons, whether or not the duty was military or administrative."[103] Thus, it was not unheard of for women to play leading military roles. In this context, a handful of women from prominent families led their own armies, and many more from all rungs of society took up arms and joined the guerilla war.[104]

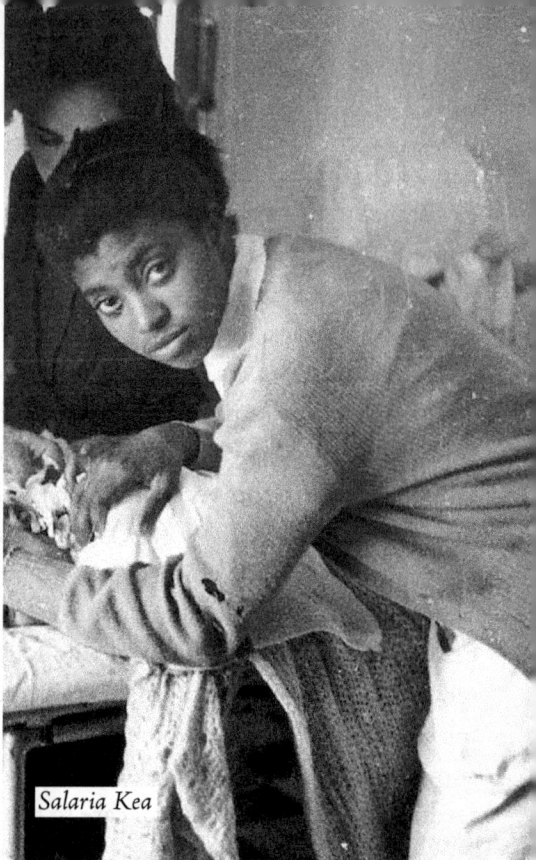

Salaria Kea

The anti-fascist/anti-colonial struggle in Ethiopia caused ripples far beyond its borders. In the United States, Mussolini's invasion sparked protests, riots, and solidarity campaigns throughout the country. Massive demonstrations took place in New York and Chicago, street fights broke out between Black anti-fascists and Italian pro-fascists, pickets were held outside of the Italian consulate, leaflets were distributed, dock workers refused to load Italian ships, and fundraising drives were organized. Black Communists set up the Joint Committee for the Defense of Ethiopia and along with other Pan-African groups spearheaded these activities. Crabapple notes, "black Americans recognized the dangers of Fascism abroad early... They saw Mussolini's Blackshirts reflected in the white hoods of the Klan, and Hitler's Jew-baiting mirrored by the systemic violence of Jim Crow."[105]

Women in the American Communist Party spoke out against

the threat fascism posed to women's rights and with the invasion of
Ethiopia sought to develop a cross-racial alliance to build class solidarity against fascism, and with varying degrees of success, worked
with Black organizations to build support for Ethiopia.[106] In Britain,
Black rights and anti-colonial activists formed the International
African Friends of Abyssinia (IAFA) to promote resistance to fascism
in Ethiopia.[107] Black radicals in America, Britain, and elsewhere drew
connections between the fight for Ethiopia and their own experiences,
as well as putting forth analyses of anti-fascism rooted in Black internationalism, anti-colonialism, and anti-imperialism.[108] Several members of the Abraham Lincoln Brigade* came to Spain as a result of their
activism in support of Ethiopia. For example, Salaria Kea—the only
Black women in the Brigade—fundraised for Ethiopian hospitals, and
when her application to join the Ethiopian army was rejected she sailed
for Spain.[109]

In July of 1936, General Francisco Franco initiated a military
rebellion against Spain's Republican government. The instigators anticipated a swift victory. However, the coup d'état was met with a spontaneous uprising, and Spain was thrown into civil war. In many of the
besieged cities, everyday civilians raided local armories, requisitioned
weapons, and took up arms to fight against the fascists. During these
early days of popular resistance, women took part in the storming of
barracks to obtain weapons, built barricades, and participated in armed
street fighting.[110] Beyond a fight against fascism, the Spanish Civil War
was also a highly contested fight for revolution. Anarchists and dissi-
dent Marxists sought to combine the anti-fascist fight with the fight for
broader revolutionary change, while communists and socialists rejected
such positions, arguing for the necessity of engaging in the war exclusively in terms of anti-fascism. This conflict led to what Nash refers to

---

* Organized by the Communist International, the Abraham Lincoln Brigade was
the battalion of volunteers from the United States who traveled to Spain to resist
fascism and fight in the civil war. Similar battalions organized by the Comintern
throughout the world were known collectively as the International Brigades.

as a "civil war within the civil war."[111] In this context, women essentially found themselves in a struggle on three fronts—fighting against fascism, fighting to push antifascist forces towards a revolutionary orientation, and then finally, fighting to make revolutionary forces take gender liberation seriously. In response, women's organizations were founded to aid the anti-fascist cause while promoting ideas of revolutionary change that included women's emancipation.

Founded a few short months before the official outbreak of the Civil War, Mujeres Libres (Free Women) was an anarchist organization that sought to contest women's subordination and mobilize women to take part in the struggle against fascism. Beginning with just a few hundred members, its numbers soared during the war, eventually reaching a membership ranging from 20,000 to 60,000 women.[112] Members of the organization were active in all aspects of the Civil War, from fighting on the front lines, as well as aiding the wounded, to maintaining collective kitchens and organizing schools for refugees and engaging in political debate.

Central to Mujeres Libres, and what made them unique, was an emphasis on organizational autonomy. The founding members of Mujeres Libres were all militants in the broader anarcho-syndicalist movement who "found the existing organizations of that movement inadequate to address the specific problems confronting them as women, whether in the movement itself or in the larger society."[113] The organization was built on the belief that women needed separate organizations to address their specific needs and, ultimately, to build their capacities to intervene and shape the political landscape. To this end, the organization took on a variety of initiatives, including: the publication of a regular newspaper aimed at political consciousness-raising; the running of classes to overcome illiteracy; the facilitation of discussion groups to challenge ignorance; the opening of women's health clinics; and the offering of industrial and commercial apprenticeships.[114] Political instruction and basic education sought to help in addressing women's cultural and sexual subordination, and professional training aimed to aid women in their economic subordination by increasing employment opportunities.

In addition to challenging women's subordination, the organization's initiatives were aimed at recruiting women into the anti-fascist movement and creating a conscious force of women who were prepared for the "social revolution." To build this force, the organization emphasized two interrelated goals and corresponding programs: *capacitación* and *captación*. The first, capacitación, was concerned with "preparing women for revolutionary engagement." Related to the educational and consciousness-raising activities outlined above, capacitación focused on the empowerment of women such that they would feel confident in their abilities, recognize their potential, and ultimately conceptualize "themselves as competent historical actors." This emphasis on personal development, individual growth, and building capacity was the result of conceptualizing struggle not only in quantitative terms, but also in qualitative ones. Moving to the second program, captación was concerned with "actively incorporating them [women] into the libertarian movement."[115] In practice, this entailed working to increase women's participation in other, larger revolutionary organizations. As Mujeres Libres worked with women to address their everyday material needs, they created the conditions necessary to bring more of them into the fold of revolutionary politics.

By the spring of 1941, the Kingdom of Yugoslavia was occupied and partitioned off by Axis forces. A portion of the country was occupied by German troops, while other areas were occupied by Bulgarian, Hungarian, and Italian troops, and Croatia was established as a Nazi puppet state ruled by a local fascist militia. In response, a Communist-led resistance movement emerged and the National Liberation Army (NLA) was formed.[116] From the outset and continuing for the duration of the conflict, women played a huge part in the partisan resistance movement. In the words of one scholar: "The mass participation of women in the communist-led Yugoslav Partisan resistance is one of the most remarkable phenomena of the Second World War."[117] Similarly, Bonfiglioli describes women's contribution as "unprecedented in Europe," explaining that "out of a population of sixteen million…[official records] report one hundred thousand women fighting as partisans, and two million participating in various ways to support the National Liberation Movement. It has been calculated that approximately twenty-five thousand women died in battle, and some two thousand women attained officer's rank."[118]

While noteworthy, women's contribution as fighters is only one part of a much bigger picture. Women participated in the anti-fascist struggle in a variety of different ways. Acting autonomously, women led food riots in face of the widespread hunger caused by the country's food stock being exported to the Third Reich.[119] Otherwise disconnected, peasant women passed information to partisans on enemy troop movements and spies, as well as harvesting crops for neighbours who were at the front or in prison. In addition to taking care of important agricultural work, many of these women also tended to wounded partisan soldiers, took care of orphans, and housed those on the run.[120] As part of organizations and collectives officially connected to the resistance movement, women took on many more roles still.

Shortly after the formation of the National Liberation Army, the Antifascist Front of Women (AFZ) was established. A specifically women's organization, the AFZ was founded as an organ of the Yugoslav Communist Party and was charged with the two-fold mission of mobilizing "large masses of women in the struggle against the German occupation and in support of the combat and noncombat activities of the Liberation Movement."[121] Anti-fascist women's committees were formed in towns, villages, and cities across the country, and members canvassed both liberated and non-liberated territories to recruit new women into the organization.[122] Once members, the work taken on by the women was all-encompassing and ranged from typical gendered tasks such as sewing and laundry, to espionage and sabotage. The women knitted socks and sweaters, sewed uniforms, and made shoes for the troops, as well as mended and laundered their clothes. They collected food, clothing, medical supplies, money, arms, and ammunition.[123] They prepared hideouts for partisans on the run, "looked after the families of the arrested and organized prison escapes."

Women acted as couriers, transporting important messages, outlawed literature, attack orders, weapons, and explosives throughout the country. They printed underground newspapers, published and distributed clandestine anti-fascist publications, and ran illegal radio stations. They dug up streets to inhibit the movement of fascist tanks and served as guards in liberated villages.[124] Women destroyed roads and rail lines, cut telephone lines, blew up power stations and other strategic targets, and burned enemy crops. They were also engaged directly at the front as nurses, cooks, and armed fighters.[125]

Local AFZ councils ran hospitals and orphanages, set up public kitchens, and organized accommodations for refugees.[126] They engaged in constructive, socially useful projects to provide much needed services and care. In addition to building women's involvement in the resistance movement, the organization agitated for women's rights and to facilitate political education.[127] The AFZ had the mission to help transform women into equal and deserving citizens of the future socialist state.[128] Specifically, this meant working to "eliminate illiteracy among women, 'raise' their political consciousness, and train them professionally" so that they could effectively participate in the process of building socialism.[129] To this end, the organization carried out a comprehensive literacy campaign offering courses that taught reading and writing in urban as well as rural areas. Along with literacy courses, the AFZ held general education classes on topics such as hygiene and health, first aid, and other practical skills.[130] Special political courses were offered for more "advanced" members and covered discussions of politics, economics, history, and culture. Working in tandem with the courses, the AFZ released publications "which, besides being tools for the dissemination of propaganda, featured educational pieces and political texts in a simple, accessible language."[131] This is a limited account—a small handful of examples from a much larger history. Nonetheless, these examples are powerful and offer lessons, inspiration, and other takeaways for anti-fascist resistance in our present moment. To explore this further, the next section considers some of the key insights that can be garnered from these histories.

Night of Resistance

March and Rally!

March 9, 1994
5:00 PM

STATE BUILDING
Van Ness & McAllister

Days of Defense

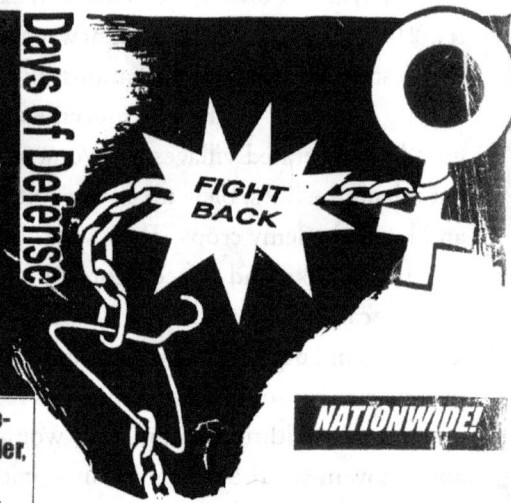

FIGHT BACK

NATIONWIDE!

On March 9, 1994, the eve of the one-year anniversary of Dr. Gunn's murder, there will be an outpouring of resistance to these attacks against women's rights and freedoms. This action will demonstrate and delcare that we will not tolerate assaults on women or abortion providers, and that we are going on the offensive to stop them.

Dr. David Gunn gave his life to bring abortions to women. Despite being disabled from childhood polio, he staffed eight clinics in three Southern states, driving long hours from one clinic to another. He carried a bullhorn in his car, and challenged the anti-abortion bigots when he arrived at a clinic that was under seige. He blasted out the song "I won't back down" and refused to be intimidated.

HIS SPIRIT AND EXAMPLE NEEDS TO BE SPREAD AND EMULATED!

The anti-abrtionists must be given no peace; they should not be allowed to meet and plan their attacks; they must be exposed and stopped! Join us in commemorating the spirit of Dr. Gunn and in renewing our commitment around the country: plan creative and powerful actions that will "light up the night" and deliver a strong message to the anti-women gangs and their backers in high places.

Brought to you by the Fight Back Network

For more information contact:
BACORR   *Refuse and Resist!*

Part 3—Learning from Our Predecessors: Towards a Feminist Antifa

We conspire; we breathe together. We share what we have been gifted to us by those who came before us. We attempt to walk beside each other. But what will we carry over with us past the emancipatory horizons we'll approach together? What histories will inform our collective actions? What energies of solidarity and creativity will animate these movements.[132]

Invoking the history of women's participation in anti-fascism, a number of lessons can be drawn and carried into our current moment. While the uncritical introduction of organizing models and ideas from other places and times is problematic, it can be useful to draw inspiration and take insights from elsewhere. History certainly does not hold all of the answers, but it can be a place (one amongst many) to start. Akemo and Busk, discussing anarchism, insist that building "an anarchist feminist historical tradition will give us a platform to advance our own politics, understand our work in the context of what has already been done, and then forge ahead… We have always existed, but we have not always been seen."[133] The same can be said for an anti-fascist feminist historical tradition. With this in mind, I propose seven general insights that can be teased out from the history of women's anti-fascist resistance and applied to contemporary anti-fascist struggles. These are not intended to be universal or prescriptive, but merely contextual and suggestive.

First, conceptualize anti-fascist resistance broadly and engage in multi-layered struggle. Embrace a variety of organizing strategies and tactics, and move away from the tendency to look at anti-fascist struggle in terms of a hierarchical ranking in which certain forms of activity (e.g., combat/fighting, involvement in formal political organizations, etc.) are placed at the top, and all other forms of activity are seen as secondary and less important. Anti-fascist resistance isn't just one thing. It involves a lot of different types of activities and requires a diversity of things. Describing the range of activities that anti-fascists historically engaged in, Bravo notes that while armed resistance and the ideal of a "young, healthy, tough, and preferably male" body were disproportionality glorified, there was also space for unarmed resistance where "the human frame was far less strictly defined" and "one could be old, weak, physically inept, sickly, and still useful and not excluded." Resistance was lived everyday by many different bodies, from those who took up arms and fought Nazis to those who engaged in sabotage, to those who aided clandestine activities, to those who fed and clothed those resisting. It encompassed both formal and informal involvement, as well as individual and collective actions. It took place in both the public and the private spheres, included physical confrontation, public education, labour and community organizing, surveillance and information gathering, the building of infrastructure, and so much more.

Building on the first, the second insight is related to the task of building an anti-fascist political culture. Calls to develop a "physical culture of class combat"[134] or to form "ultras" football supporter clubs[135] are fine, but limited.* If we want to develop a strong resistance movement, we cannot focus almost exclusively on physical activities and/or traditionally male-dominated spaces.** It's important to have spaces, roles, and activities that account for the variety and diversity of social life—for example, considering things like ability and age. Historically,

---

* As part of this, I would also include the aggrandizement of particular aesthetics. It's fine to be into a certain style or subculture, but they can present limits. A sleek Adidas sports jacket; a crisp Fred Perry polo shirt, etc.—at least in some spaces anti-fascism has a particular European influenced aesthetic. Inherited from the white-dominated punk subcultures from which modern antifa emerged, this aesthetic can function to hinder struggle if anti-fascism is exclusively thought of or associated with a specific dress code. Aesthetics should not be a stand-in for, nor should it be prioritized over, politics.

** Anti-fascist gyms are great, and anti-fascist football clubs can be useful. But what about an anti-fascist neighbourhood association? Or anti-fascist storytelling time for children, or an anti-fascist food program? Or maybe, anti-fascist day at the nail salon or an anti-fascist roller derby league? The list could go on.

there existed a wide range of anti-fascist cultural spaces. These included things like reading groups, social clubs, collective kitchens, daycare centers, workplace organizations, and sports associations.

Thirdly, the next insight concerns the propensity to associate particular types of activity with particular types of bodies. Against the tendency to associate women with passivity and non-violence, it is crucial to recognize that combative politics is not exclusively the domain of men. Throughout the history of anti-fascist resistance and continuing today, women, queers, and trans folk have been involved in armed uprisings, self-defense initiatives, physical confrontations, coordinated attacks, and various other forms of violent activity. Critiquing such actions as inherently male and exclusionary to all others, marginalizes the diverse voices of those engaged in confrontational tactics, and furthermore, perpetuates restrictive gender stereotypes.

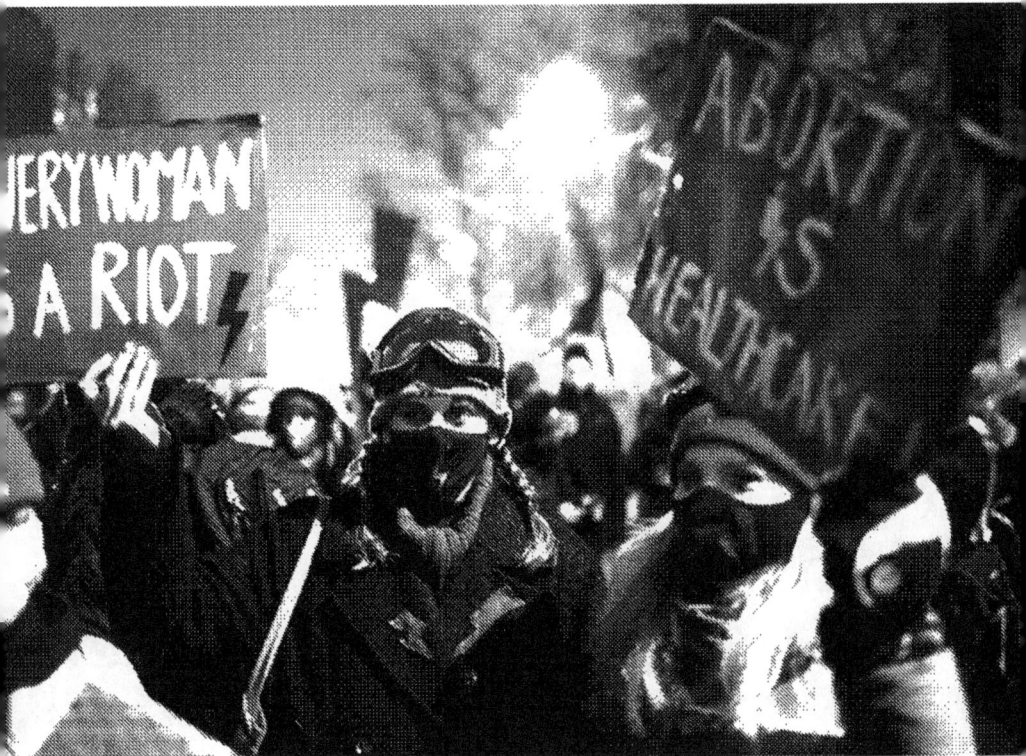

That said, it is also true that anti-fascism has issues with sexism and patriarchal behaviour, and "that whenever confrontation is part of the repertoire, it is an extra concern."[136] Which leads to the fourth insight: couple anti-fascist politics with feminism and conceptualize gender liberation as a non-negotiable component of anti-fascism. This means centering gender considerations and taking trans politics and queer struggle seriously, not treating them as peripheral concerns. Relatedly, the fifth insight concerns the value of autonomy and autonomous organizing. Creating autonomous spaces and/or pushing for organizational autonomy were crucial to many historical anti-fascist groups. Many women found themselves in a situation where they were fighting against fascism and fighting for revolutionary change, all the while pushing their movements to take gender oppression seriously. To

Photo Credit: Peg Hunter

address this layered struggle, women founded separate organizations to undertake the work that was otherwise brushed off.

Sixth, look to and draw on other anti-racist and anti-colonial resistance traditions and not just those most commonly associated with anti-fascism. Popular accounts of anti-fascist history privilege Europe and disproportionately focus on white actors. The proto-typical anti-fascist hero is presented not only as male but also as white, ignoring all other histories. There is an incredibly long legacy of Black and Indigenous struggle; however, these are often overlooked and go unrecognized. Jegroo notes: "While many people think of white anarchists... punching Nazis when they talk about antifa, Black folks in the Western hemisphere have essentially been doing antifascist work for centuries. It just hasn't been recognized as such."[137] Particularly in North America—a continent defined by settler colonialism, Indigenous genocide, and anti-Blackness—Black liberation and decolonial movements have either explicitly or implicitly been engaged in fighting against fascism for hundreds of years.* Even though much of this work wasn't done under the label of anti-fascist, that doesn't make it any less relevant. These histories and their continuation today are crucial to conceptualizing and engaging in anti-fascist struggle.

Moving to the final point, the last insight is to connect anti-fascism with more ambitious revolutionary goals. Anti-fascism in and of itself is a necessarily limited struggle. It is a reactive and defensive movement that, while incredibly important, is much more of a jumping off point than a desired final destination. In the past, many groups rooted their anti-fascist work in a commitment to revolution and pushed for

---

* There are countless examples. Before the height of the civil rights movement, Black activists like Mabel and Robert Williams worked to arm Black people and taught them how to defend themselves against the Ku Klux Klan. The Black Panthers held a national conference in 1969 on anti-fascism (the National Revolutionary Conference for a United Front Against Fascism). Many Black intellectuals have theorized the role of fascism in America, and also done much to highlight (and organize against) police as key perpetrators of fascist violence.

a broader vision of collective liberation and societal transformation. Anti-fascism wasn't a single struggle, but an overlapping set of struggles taking place simultaneously. It was an anti-fascist war, but also a civil war and a class war fighting for sweeping social, political, and economic change.

Conclusion: Against Machismo, For Militancy

> Part of making anti-fascist politics stronger means con-
> tending with the hyper-masculinity and predominant
> whiteness of antifa spaces... Rather than be dismissed as
> secondary issues that fall behind the primary goal of con-
> fronting fascists, disability justice, anti-racism, and femin-
> ism should be at the forefront of any revolutionary analysis...
> This also means recognizing that anti-fascism is a necessary
> but insufficient political solution to the problems of our
> time.[138]

Misogyny is a fundamental pillar of contemporary far-right politics; it is not just an aside. With the proliferation of far-right movements over the last few years, and more recently with the recuperation of those movements and their abhorrent ideas by political parties and ruling institutions, it is crucial to understand all that we are up against. Part of what we face is the growth of political forces shaped by variations of intensely patriarchal ideology, and as such, forces that aspire to establish (or rather further establish, more accurately) not just white supremacy, but white male supremacy. This reality desperately calls for a response— it is a growing nightmare that is all too quickly becoming normalized— and the only appropriate response is struggle. Unfortunately, the ready-made options presented to us leave much to be desired. On the one hand, liberal feminism fundamentally lacks the teeth to address our current political climate, leading to a dead end of permitted marches, electoral campaigns, and "pussy hat" politics. On the other hand, anti-fascism is plagued by machismo, leading to a highly reductive understanding of struggle and the glorification hyper-masculine activities above all else. Anti-fascism doesn't have to be that way—we can do better.

Looking to histories of women's participation in anti-fascist movements, we can catch glimpses of a different anti-fascism. Contrary to the common conception, women were involved in all forms and formations of the historical fight against fascism. Ingrid Strobl paints a vibrant picture; referencing women's involvement in anti-fascist activities, she explains:

> They were activists in urban brigades, the ghetto underground, and partisan units. They printed and distributed the illegal press; they forged papers; they transported weapons and themselves participated in armed actions. They organized underground movements and ghetto uprisings; they were political cadres and military commanders of groups. [They engaged in sabotage]. They found hiding places for Jewish children and youth, brought them to these hiding places, provided them with clothing, money, food, and with forged documents and encouragement over months and sometimes years.[139]

There is a lot of inspiration and many lessons that can be taken from this history. This is not to say that all aspects of these histories are applicable to our current situation—we are struggling in a vastly different context. However, there are valuable takeaways, as were explored above, and these takeaways offer solid ground on which to build an anti-fascism rooted in revolutionary feminism. Against an anti-fascism shaped by machismo, a revolutionary feminist anti-fascism is shaped by the concept of militancy. Before discussing the latter, it is useful to look at the former.

There is a thread that flows through anti-fascist movements, and while it does not exclusively define contemporary anti-fascism, it is influential and worth noting. The thread is an orientation/attitude that tends towards machismo. This inclination is one of bravado and dogmatic combativity, and leads to a political position that prioritizes confrontation while it more or less ignores (or at least downplays) other aspects of struggle. It reproduces some of the worst characteristics of hegemonic masculinity with a self-righteous zeal, and considers discussion of things like sexism to be needlessly divisive and a distraction from the "important things." This strain is almost exclusively concerned with physical conflict with fascists, where if you aren't willing or able to "throw down," you aren't an anti-fascist. It is individualistic and leans towards an orientation of doing what one wants, regardless of the consequences. It is concerned more with the act of the fight itself than it is with the outcome. There is no room for nuance or any consideration of context, and strategy largely falls by the wayside.* These characteristics can be described as machismo, and an anti-fascism rooted in machismo is the political equivalent of a bar fight—as haphazard and chaotic as it is incoherent and often sloppy.**

In contrast, an anti-fascism oriented towards militancy instead of machismo is concerned with commitment, collectivity, and effectiveness. It isn't about image or ego; rather, it is about doing what needs to be done, choosing the methods/tactics best suited for a situation, and looking at the bigger liberatory picture. This approach couples anti-fascist politics with feminism and conceptualizes gender liberation as a

---

* For example, there's no distinction made between different tendencies on the right, everyone from a self-identified neo-Nazi to christian conservatives is a fascist and must be confronted in the same manner.

** I mostly mean this figuratively, but I also know lots of examples of dudes going out drinking to the bar and purposefully looking for fascists to fight. In this case, there literally is an "anti-fascist bar fight." This usually looks like men who identify as anti-fascist getting into a bar fight with those perceived to be fascists, though this sometimes get muddled (e.g., is the guy wearing that t-shirt of a fascist metal band actually a fascist, or does he just like the band and not know anything about its politics?).

non-negotiable component of anti-fascism. Such politics starts from the understanding that anti-fascist resistance isn't just one thing—it involves a lot of different types of activities and a large diversity of roles. A vibrant movement would have a place for a two-year-old child up to their eighty-two-year-old grandparent. This does not mean a move away from street politics, confrontational tactics, or the use of violence; it acknowledges that antagonism and conflict are inherent to anti-fascist politics and that confrontation/violence is both necessary and justifiable in certain circumstances. It also acknowledges that women, queers, and trans folk do often "throw down" and are involved in physical altercations and other confrontational activities. Thus, there is an emphasis on dispelling the gendered myth that only men engage in such activities.

Beyond recognizing the role of combative politics, there is also an emphasis on expanding the number of people who participate in confrontational moments, and thus in putting effort into building the comfort and capacity for more women and queers to take part in those activities that are usually coded as hyper-masculine. While it values these activities, an anti-fascism that is rooted in militancy rather than machismo knows that violence is not appropriate in all situations, and that the habit of narrowly focusing on physical confrontations is detrimental to our movements. Fighting isn't winning—there's a lot more to it than that. Even in the example of street violence, there's more to it than just fighting. There's a lot of background work involved, including intelligence gathering, neighbourhood organizing, logistical planning, and legal/prison support.

This work, which is usually feminized, is as valuable as the confrontational activities it supports. It's just that the one type of work isn't particularly sexy and is perpetually undervalued, while the other is exciting and easily glorified. A feminist anti-fascism does it all and values it all; it knows that the unglamorous and boring work plays an essential part in struggle. Of related importance, an anti-fascism rooted in militancy considers both the qualitative and quantitative sides of struggle. This means it isn't just concerned with how many fascist rallies it shuts down, but also with the subjective experience and the personal development of those involved. Ideally, people are learning skills, developing confidence, and becoming more capable revolutionaries. Beyond the immediate benefits, these developments will be helpful for other struggles moving forward. The infrastructure and abilities we build, and the resources we develop, should be part of and put to use by broader struggles. Our anti-fascist organizing should be grounded in revolutionary politics, in pushing for a vision of collective liberation, meaningful autonomy, and endless possibility. The problems we face are so much bigger than the question of fascism, and our aspirations should be so much more than this limited struggle.

On Reading Anti-Fascism Against Machismo

Butch Lee, December 9, 2019

This is exciting. Because it starts to break away from the once fresh but increasingly dead end of what had become macho *antifa*.

There's not only false gender assumptions involved, but white racism stirred in here. Some white people always want to think that fascism is a white issue they own. That it's evil white men, only being overcome by good white men. More white patriarchy coming and going. *Anti-Fascism Against Machismo* goes for it, in kicking out this kind of dusty old politics.

Realize that many readers aren't going to understand fully what and why i'm saying unless this is put out on the kitchen table. i'm a cranky 80-year-old-white woman. Born just as the big World War II was starting. So growing up, everyone talked about the war against fascism. Fighting the nazis and all. Adults had done it, children played at it. We never thought fascism was a problem growing up. Hadn't the nazis been killed? Defeated, wiped out? Fascism was permanently finished, to us.

That childhood was in a small town in New Jersey. Not a suburb, where the husbands commute to the big city to work every day. A town, where most people lived and worked locally. Across the street was the family of a house painter. While the railroad yard worker and the milkman were several other fathers on the block. My father, a local accountant, was successful as our white neighborhood went. White women didn't have jobs outside the household in our time and there. On our street

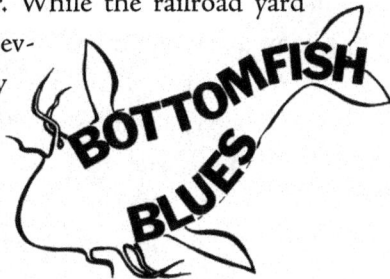

the only woman who knew how to drive a car was the school teacher. Whose husband was disabled. White women didn't have an independent income or independent transportation. Or own the house they and their children lived in. Their husbands did. That was our real lives, while what Margaret Atwood writes is science-fiction. Right?

Many places like our restaurants didn't allow Jewish customers inside. But it wasn't an issue since there were no Jews there at all. Except the hidden Jews, like my mother. But we were white and didn't understand it. Since there were no Black families around us or ever any in our schools. Knew that there were Black people. But just thought of them as far away with their own lives and problems. Like what we unknowingly were mistaught to call "Eskimos". Didn't seem to be anything we needed to think about. Yes, hard as it is to believe, i came into teen years and left home, still unaware. Of lynchings, Jim Crow, segregation or anything. That wasn't the story on the ground when i first came to the battles. There wasn't much TV yet. Not that Black people were on TV. So what little you saw in person, you thought was what there was.

When i was 17 having finished one freshman year and two sophomore years at high school. My moms seeing that finishing high school wasn't in my future, engineered my escape to Chicago. Which was the city of my dreams. i'd found cheap paperback novels at the bus terminal, with lurid colorful covers. In them it was a sinful big city with jazz players and bohemians. Criminals daylighting as factory workers. People of color and misfit queer exiles from all over. And to my satisfaction, it turned out to be just true enough.

Looking back, it sounds like i had a mix of teenage white cultural tourism. With a shot of survival desperation. That's what it was, too. Didn't know any better then.

A few years later there, i was coming down 53rd Street one day. Came up to the Woolworth's 5 & dime store with its big red sign. There was some kind of picketing going on, with stuff being shouted. A tall blond guy bounced over to intercept me. Handing me a flyer about supporting the southern Black student sit-ins, a new idea just starting to spread. He exclaimed dramatically (as i later learned he did everything), *"You should be in the civil rights movement!"* When i confessed that i didn't know what any of this was about, his face lit up. A chance to educate a newbie on the terrible racist evils going on. By nightfall i was in the young civil rights movement. And as they say, it was all propinquity from there. (BTW, that tall charismatic boy turned out to find his own rebellion in London. Where he became a muckraking film maker. And later the chairman of something called WikiLeaks).

i was unexpectedly in a movement not my own that swept a major poor neighborhood. Attracting everyone, like older teens who grew their own herb in vacant lots for selling on the street in nickel bags. To older women who were union veterans of back-breaking assembly lines and bureaucratic betrayals. Mothers and unofficial sages. Instead of reading newspaper headlines, our illegal actions *were* the newspaper headlines. It was exciting and empowering.

But what i wasn't dealing with, is that i was taking a free ride. In a struggle that hadn't cost me a single thing. While so many others had paid heavily. People tried to educate me, though i wasn't absorbing it any too smartly. Always remember an older Black man who ran a little store near the Cabrini Green housing projects. We used to talk, and he told me how the preachers who were leading the demonstrations couldn't be trusted. And how the "integration" that was the official civil rights goal wasn't going to be what we thought. Once, seeing how confused i was, he told me gently that i sure didn't know anything about race. But that someday i would understand.

White socialist and anarchist men i came to know talked about fascism sometimes. But in a kinda abstract way. It was interesting intellectual stuff. Not any real problem on their agenda. The first people to me saying fascism was a real problem was the Black nation. Some calling out that it was urgent. Of course, they were the ones getting killed. To the Black movement then fascism was more of an actual presence shadowing all our futures.

So then, in the 1960s antifascism in the u.s. came to many of us from a Black thing. Something many white people don't know about. Although the "f" word had been widely and loosely used by all kinds of rebels then. The main start at organizing antifascism came from the Black Panther Party. Who drew 5,000 young militants to their July 1969 United Front Against Fascism conference in Oakland, California. The Panthers became popular teachers in trying to analyze fascism. Not as old European history. But in terms of the America we were being forced to fight head on.

Petronella Lee* herself brings this up in the zine. About how Black people and Indigenous peoples and many others had been fighting something like fascism here from the start. One of the reasons her perspective is a needed reframing of the issue.

The Black Panther Party saw fascism through a Black lens. As

---

* Editor's Note: The original version of "Anti-Fascism Against Machismo" was published as a zine, written pseudonymously be "Petronella Lee."

THE BLACK PANTHER

Black Community News Service

25 cents

VOL. 3 NO. 8

SATURDAY, MAY 31, 1969

PUBLISHED WEEKLY

THE BLACK PANTHER PARTY

MINISTRY OF INFORMATION
BOX 2967, CUSTOM HOUSE
SAN FRANCISCO, CA 94126

FASCISM in America

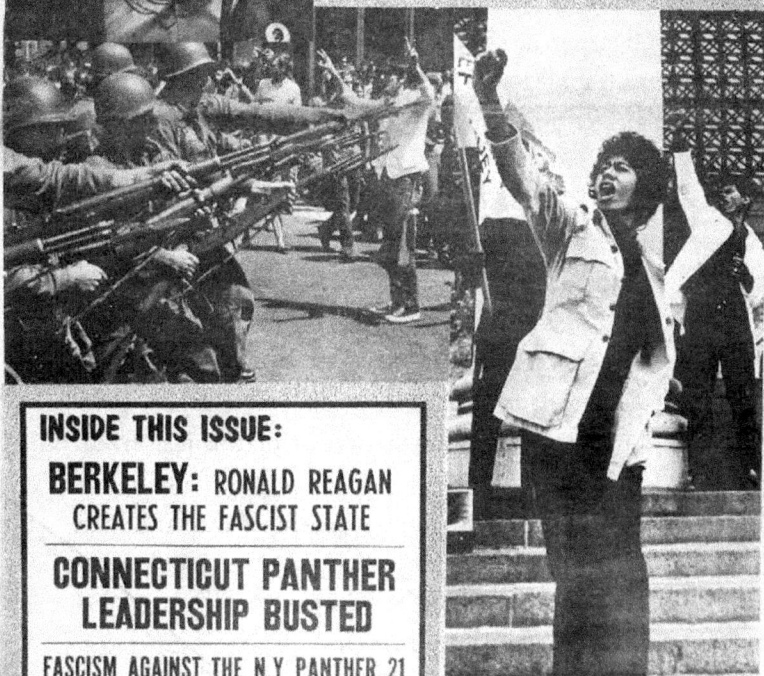

INSIDE THIS ISSUE:

BERKELEY: RONALD REAGAN CREATES THE FASCIST STATE

CONNECTICUT PANTHER LEADERSHIP BUSTED

FASCISM AGAINST THE N.Y PANTHER 21

ERICKA HUGGINS
WIFE OF THE LATE JOHN JEROME HUGGINS

a tightening white police state directly ruled by a tightening elite of only the few largest corporations. A never seen before type of super-wealthy technological society. Making aggressive war on an ever widening circle of invaded peoples of color in countries all over the world. Covered up by an artificial consumeristic way of life. Pretend governed by two faked political parties play-acting at democracy. To them it was like a dense cake of sure enough fascism baking hot below the surface. Covered all over with a sweet white race icing. These first approximations at a relevant to here analysis had both XL size insights and XL size misunderstandings. Which might not be too different from us now.

In general, the Black liberation movement then tried coming to grips with fascism differently. As something not as different from but similar to "Americanism" itself. Fascism sounded a helluva lot like what Black people had been fighting to get out from under, their whole lives after all. The Black Panther program for fighting fascism was people uniting on fighting "fascist pig" police repression in every way necessary. Calling on the abolition of big city and small town police departments alike even before a final revolution. Replacing capitalist state policing entirely with community based conflict control. And power in their own communities. Something tragically prophetic in light of today's devastating mass incarceration. With the attempted starting all over again differently of Black Lives Matter.

As action makes reaction, the extreme police repression of 1960s Black liberation led to an extreme resistance. Something like the days of the 1860s Black land pirates only with revolutionary politics. Those were spontaneous outlaw organizations of the just freed but with nothing. Operating violently in the temporary no-man's zone of lost Confederate territory bypassed by quickly advancing Union armies. (Their favorite targets were the "rich" Union supply wagon convoys, and they could take no prisoners.) In the 1970s, small groups first of surviving Black Panthers and their close comrades, made a new armed underground. To take the war back to the police. Financed by bank expropriations. Named the Black Liberation Army. Lasting little more than a decade, it never was large. It was more of a widely shared concept of all-out illegal resistance than any set organization. But it changed the parameters of politics. This wasn't the civil rights movement anymore.

In like way, the system's mass incarceration has led inevitably to extreme inside resistance. Through the ups and downs of political struggles in the u.s.a., the prison movement has built visible calls for the actual dismantling of the capitalist carceral system of injustice. With mass hunger strikes involving well-known inmates. Prison-wide work stoppages. Their voices at great sacrifice reach over capitalist walls.

Overall, the 1960s failure at revolutionary change in the highest level was historically tragic. Here and all over the oppressed post-colonial periphery. Which we could see in the wrecks of male-centered, authoritarian liberation that didn't work.

Fascism/antifascism alike, there's a new deal of the cards.

What i think of as second-wave fascism, we first ran up against in the 1950s-1960s. They were fixated on anti-Black race hatred job one. On re-establishing traditional popular white dictatorship over Black and other oppressed peoples. Who were rising up, everywhere escaping colonial imprisonment. So the fascist core within the Klans and the first small neo-Nazi bands espoused being very patriotic to the old white u.s.a.

Always remember what we didn't know back in our young 1960s. That many millions of white Americans had been pro-fascist in the 1930s. Before the white sweethearts breakup with Italy and Germany at WWII. U.S. Army General Hugh Johnson, the director of President Roosevelt's National Recovery Administration against the Depression, said that he was being guided by Mussolini's fascist ideas. Ethnic community bodies like some German-American police and athletic associations endorsed Hitler after 1933. Just as the Italian-American Catholic parishes actively organized neighborhood drives to help fund Mussolini's fascist movement. White fascism and "Americanism" were bros then.

In the 1950s and 1960s, George Lincoln Rockwell had his small American Nazi Party startup. With nazi tan storm trooper garb, swastika armbands and all. Their program though was for patriotic old

THE SYMBOL OF
WHITE POWER

white America. Rockwell himself was a serving u.s. Navy officer, who fought to keep his active duty status in the u.s. government.

Strategically, we thought with most people our age then that these were just costume-wearing nasty nutcases. Outliers even within the large white racist crowd (that's the majority of the u.s. white population, we had been made painfully aware). But we were just as aware that they could still be dangerous tactically. Not a small point. One of my close comrades and friends from the early civil rights days, Wayne Yancy, was killed in Mississippi then. His death covered up as a car accident. Until people who went to his funeral in Paris, Tennessee, were told by the funeral director that his body was full of bullets. Nutcase white men could kill you just as dead as a professional CIA gunman.

Rockwell's first nazi party here never grew, but he had sown seeds that we didn't see. In 1965 he recruited a college instructor named William Pierce to fascism. Putting him to work editing and writing the tiny party's publication, *National Socialist World*. After Rockwell's death, Pierce left the dying nazi party to become the far right's most important figure. His revolutionary novel, *The Turner Diaries*, became white fascism's uniting call to battle, its bible, and its blueprint. Rockwell is invisibly present as well in the popular slogan he hit on. That is bigger than ever today: "White Power".

New third-wave fascism here has a flashy political uniform. Though it is less always leading with anti-Black issues. For several important reasons. Most tactical of which is that the white fascists are dead afraid of the Black nation. More than ever. They have an ominous idea of what might happen to them if they started trying to take their white rallies around Black communities. Let the drugged giant sleep. Better Berkeley and Manhattan for their staged far right vs. left clashes.

The other big reason is that the state has done it for them. Always busy spending billions to uneducate Black people, then unemploying them. Killing them, shrinking their land footprint every year, moving them on. Could the klan and nazis get away with killing and concentration camping as many Black people every year as the "liberal democratic" state?

But naturally the white fascists are not grateful at all. Third-wave fascism here was *"born in the u.s.a."*. Out of Vietnam defeats, forced integration, and man-abandoning feminism. It wants to overthrow the hated u.s. government of the New World Order's globalization. To win a dystopian white men's concentration camp society.

There are clearly two other races that have the most popular resonance for today's racist killers: Muslim immigrants and Indigenous peoples from Central and South America. Who are the invasion threatening white America's homeland. Who are the easiest targets. Third-wave fascist propaganda dovetails right into the traditional American Main Street. And back across the ocean to the latest far right eruptions of the European fatherland.

Petronella Lee's short zine is so exciting in that it opens a door of understanding for women. She has to start pointing us towards the upped white fascist threat to women, because few others are systematically doing it. The usual white macho *antifa* sure hasn't. It turns out that gender as well as race are central to the cutting edge of the story. And central to the larger roadmap. So *Anti-Fascism Against Machismo: gender politics and the struggle against fascism*, explains this in an urgent way.

"In the spring of 2017, a video of an anti-fascist being beaten at a counter demonstration in Berkeley went viral", she starts. It vividly showed anti-fascist demonstrator Louise Rosealma punched in the face. Knocked down by a white supremacist leader.

Not denying it, the fascists themselves spread the video. Gloried in having physically attacked a woman they designated "whore" and "traitor". Rosealma is a cisgender young white woman. Coincidentally a porn worker, she became a convenient body terrain for patriarchal right and patriarchal left to mark lines on. Memed and doxxed. Her personal info spread for hating white men to harass her with rape threats, death threats.

Same when Heather Heyer was infamously murdered in the 2017 Charlottesville protests. The fascists again proudly at first claimed her killing. One of the rally organizers called it "payback" to a "fat, disgusting communist". *The Daily Stormer* has been one of the internet fascist playgrounds. With hundreds of thousands of followers. It dismissed her killing as an act with zero consequences. Since "a 32 year old woman without children is a burden on society and has no value".

The liberal feminists and progressives who spoke out to defend Louise Rosealma showed disturbing problems of their own. Louise was spoken of as someone who should be presumed to be "nonviolent" because of her gender. Beating her was denounced as "cowardly". Implying that as a woman she must be considered weaker. Unable to defend herself. Logically built on all that crap, were the liberal feminist calls for more carceral police protection over women as the only answer for us.

This gives us the phone number of the political moment we are living in, Petronella Lee points out. Where white fascism is eager to make examples by violently targeting women as individuals. Towards targeting us eventually as an entire gender class. Where erectile capitalism tries to box in our choices to a passive "pussy hat" liberal feminism. With hapless pleas for more state protective policing. While the patriarchal left response, she notes acidly, is still dominated by "reductive anti-fascism defined by machoism and sexism".

First round fired, she is saying that this is not our grandparents' fascism. That the new upsurge of fascism at society's public edges is different. About ten years ago watchers began noticing the "Manosphere". Or the very rapidly spreading bramble of online sites and blogs rallying misogynist white men. To share and admit their bitter oppression under all the "stupid slut" feminist women who reject them. Hating women as their No. 1 personal enemy. Calling on all alienated white men to violently take back their supreme power over women. Against the politically correct feminist communist conspiracy. Lone wolf right-wing attacks and mass killings against women walked further into our news.

What Petronella isn't afraid to explore, is that women should lead our fight against fascism. Draw our own wider strategies. Make our own diversely talented groups. Because fighting fascism is a woman-centered struggle for our lives now. Antifascism is crucially about gender as well as race.

There is a wide difference between what this zine is showing us, on the one hand. Against the pruned back, censored story that the capitalist authorities are trying to keep women pacified with. Here's what i mean to say:

While starting to write this review, opened my morning newspaper to a political background article on u.s. far right violence. In Max Fisher's *The Interpreter* column from London. Which is meant to be prestigious. And says it uses "political science and social science" to "explore the ideas and context behind major world events". On August 6th, the major world trend he was explaining for us poor uneducated women was: '*White Terrorism Shows "Stunning" Parallels to Rise of Islamic State*'. So the new third-wave white fascism here is very similar to the muslim fascism of the global terrorist Islamic State? Not much of a surprise to women the world over, i'd say.[1]

Guess which word doesn't even appear once in this oh so deep article in America's most liberal newspaper? *Why, the unimportant word,* "*women*". What patriarchal capitalist experts have analyzed as "major world events" don't require our presence at all. Much less our thoughts and activity. Women are just there in the background of the capitalist patriarchy's owned biosphere. Us along with forests and elephants and the rest of nature. He and the other mostly liberal, mostly white male experts sense something "stunning", "*but you don't know what it is, do you Mr. Jones?*"

The *New York Times* dropped the other gender class shoe five days later. When on August 11th a serious reporting crew of Julie Bosman, Kate Taylor, and Tim Arango put out a major article: "*Many Gunmen in Mass Shootings Share a Hate Towards Women.*" On the plus side identifying severe misogyny as the big common element in imperialist culture's *amateur* mass killings here in Babylon. This is a mixed up bag, though.[2]

To make it clear. As opposed to the first *amateur* kind, our own society's *professional* mass killings are the now routine bombings and rocketings of civilian families. Done anywhere in the world capitalist periphery. War crimes done constantly by u.s. military planes and drones with many more casualties than any here. Large numbers of the aircraft and drone pilots doing the killing are now women. Not only servicewomen but civilian women mercenary contract employees.

Which is just the new "normal" most women here are never allowed to mentally question. Or link up in our understandings, in our mirrored imperialist culture, to the rising violence against us. But as that burning out sister warned us, *"It's all the same damn day"*.

That *Times* news analysis is on the growing terrorism of hating women. Which they try to keep separate from the assumed real terrorism of men's official politics. So instead like everything about women it is *domesticized*. Shrunk down. It's not political violence, it's "domestic violence". It's not a growing far right political hate campaign over our bodies. No, it's only the psychological problems of a few lonely misfit men. All to be fixed with better gun laws and more psychological screening. Toward the end, the journalists finally have to confess: "Experts say the same patterns that lead to the radicalization of white supremacists and other terrorists can apply to misogynists..." That's all there is, one line on the main point going forward. Which has been minimized not explained. Trying not to admit the linked commonality of what is coming down.

We can see how this subtle misinformation works: the *Times* journalists call up the example of a special "incel" hero who acted on his hatred for white women refusing to have sex with him: "Special reverence is reserved on those websites for Elliot O. Rodger, who killed six people in 2014 in Isla Vista, California. A day after posting a video titled 'Elliot Rodger's Retribution'. In it, he describes himself as being tortured by sexual deprivation and promising to punish women for rejecting him... Several mass killers have cited Mr. Rodger as an inspiration."

What's left out? A whole lot. The wide ranging article mentions him murdering, but doesn't quote his final online words to *"slaughter every single spoiled, stuck up blond slut"* on his University of California campus. A raging last will that is consistent with just how violently political his acting out was. Why some journalists labeled him the first mass killer of the alt-right.

In addition to the six murder victims they do mention, Rodger also attacked and wounded fourteen others that morning that weren't mentioned (the wounded really don't count?). More, they also didn't tell us that the *first three people he killed* were his two male Asian student apartment mates and a male Asian friend of theirs. Even though he himself was eurasian (white father and ethnic Chinese Malaysian mother), Rodger hated Asians and said they were animal-like. He also believed in the biological inferiority of Latinos and most especially Black people.

So unmentioned race hatred was right there, too. It turns out that Rodger was a nazi sympathizer, but that was left out. His internet interests included learning as much as he could about fascist heroes Hitler and the notorious S.S. chief Heinrich Himmler. Fascists must have noticed that his rampage took place on the anniversary of Heinrich Himmler's death. Although the Santa Barbara County Sheriff's office said that this was only a "coincidence". (i personally don't believe in men's "coincidences".) The term "fascism" nowhere appears in this article on the far right politically encouraging more and more violent lone wolf attacks against women. For women and for all of us, this was as political as a Donald Trump latest "personal" tweet.[3]

We get it. The patriarchal capitalist authorities want women to only know a dumbed down version of what's ugly coming towards us. A de-politicized version. They want to break it up into isolated pieces, just as women were once called only a "piece". And compartmentalize away what's happening. Recasting as individual, domestic, and psychological the news of a dangerous political shift. But never saying how it's related to the roots of fascism itself. Never admitting that these explosions they say are different kinds of terrorism, are really parts of the same damn far right fire. Where our bodies are the fuel to be consumed.

To say what Petronella Lee put together for us is a light-year ahead of all that, is an understatement. *Anti-Fascism Against Machismo* explains much more about this new far right wave. Built heavily around woman-hating that joins their formative race hatred they are better known for. As well as the more traditional patriarchal far right in America. Which still hold to the tried & true judeo-christian-islamic basic ground rules: confining women's lives mostly or even completely to the nursery, kitchen, and bedroom. She explains the spectrum of fascist sexism, the rough division into a more usual patriarchal fascism versus total misogynist fascism.

Petronella Lee explains their basic unity in the fascist philosophical mindset of "essentialism". This is not something i knew much about. Which i think many of us can say. Where everything in nature is said to have its own unique essence. Which is fixed and determines its unchangeable characteristics. White men alone are the highest level of biological nature, in this view. The sole creators and highest alpha predators. So are the only rightful commanders of the world. To use a too familiar example.

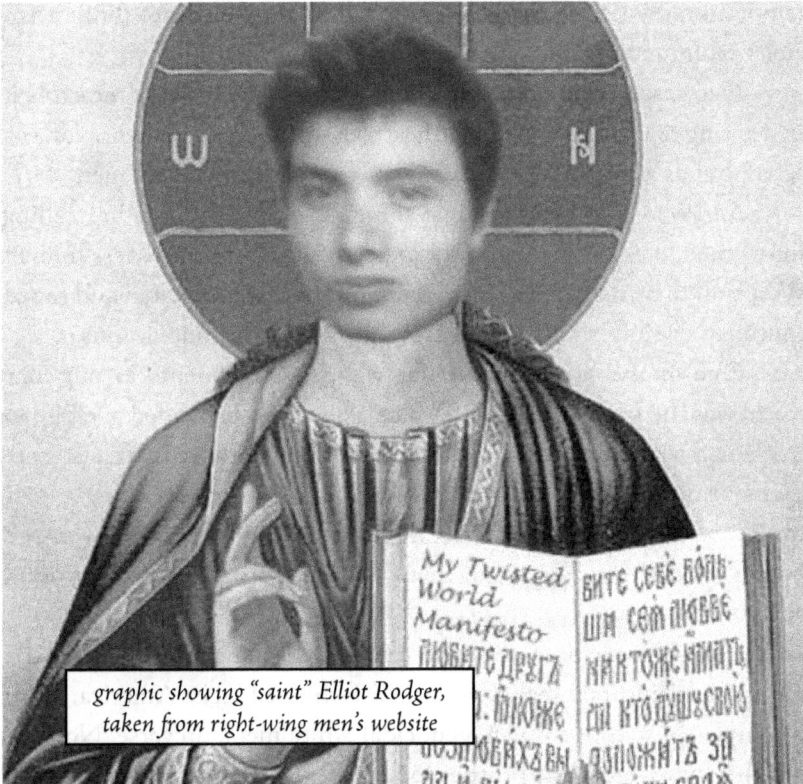

graphic showing "saint" Elliot Rodger, taken from right-wing men's website

Because of today's cultural pull from the "Manosphere", this quick to read zine dispenses with any of the many-sided discussions about how you define fascism? Instead, she says it's more immediately useful to treat it as a "process", not as one stationary defined "thing". This feels bold though incomplete, but it does look at things quickly from a different angle.

In which resentful white men are first drawn in. Intrigued, then reassured. Then captivated. In other words, being "groomed" step by step. Moving them towards fascism. So misogynist hate talk is part of the core process of today's fascism here. By the constant internet word machine-gunning of conspiracy theories. Of flattering and mocking racist and sexist resentments. By exhortations about how all white men need to be heroic in their hate. Start violently shocking superior euro-aryan male civilization back to its senses. By yielding to their deepest temptation. By letting themselves go, falling headlong into totalitarian violence. Into mass killing as a cultural building ritual.

Neo-fascist white men's voices are still proliferating. Some explicit in wanting to beat up and violently attack women. *All* women. Not as a tactic, but as a sought after new higher way of life for white men.

As Petronella Lee explains: some new white fascists are calling for women to be permanently subjugated without rights as less human. We are all to be denied free movement on the streets. Beaten and raped routinely, or simply killed after using, as men's discipline over us.

One of the breakthrough far rightist experiments in our new world was the Islamic Califate. Which explosively expanded itself up in Iraq and Syria. From being a small startup into a large temp fascist state. Doing it not in years but in only months. Suddenly occupying a territory larger than England. With millions of legally enslaved women's bodies for them to assign and then reassign. To sell and trade around and consume up.

Third-wave white fascists here want to be like that. To replace the messy multicultural breakdown of old-fashioned racist America. With a completely stripped down, genocidal white men's universe. No wonder they have had a felt brotherhood with the islamic fascists. Which went public right after the universal attention-grabbing 9/11 World Trade Center and Pentagon airplane attacks. As the third-wave white fascists then applauded the mass killings and envied. It's on the record. That's who they are.[4]

In her part 2, Against Heroes, Petronella Lee goes on being just as perceptive for us. She calls this section that because she insists we have to interrupt the *antifa* narrative we have always been given. That's the heroic men's tale that is always just assumed to be true. That while romanticizing a few women, is always shrinking, domesticizing, marginalizing the whole of women's own rising against fascism. For there has never been antifascism ever without the militant participation of women. But women have been scrubbed from his-story, so that new women always have to try and reinvent our wheel all over again.

She calls this part "an incomplete history of women's anti-fascist resistance". Her intent is to "provide a snapshot of a history too frequently forgotten and in the process, challenge the dominant image of the anti-fascist hero." Which is not "an armed partisan woman, but a generic anti-racist skinhead dude or perhaps the anti-fascist man as depicted in classic propaganda posters with rifle, sickle, and hammer in hand."

To show truer dimensions of women fighting against fascism, Lee goes to the large-scale experiences of women engaged in the wars against the world-threatening European fascism of the 1930s and 1940s. Not where we might expect, though.

She steps around old Hollywood clichés and stereotypes. Using women's fighting in lesser known to us here antifascist fronts: against Italian fascism's colonial invasion of Ethiopia in 1935; against General Franco's 1936 far right army revolt in Spain, which was aided by nazi Germany and Mussolini's Italy; and most surprisingly, against the 1941 invasion and occupation of Yugoslavia by the fascists during WWII.

Surprising because it was maybe the largest most of us haven't heard about. A historian she quotes writes that it was *"unprecedented"*. Because *"out of a population of sixteen million"*, they had *"one hundred thousand women fighting as partisans, and two million participating in*

antifascist women's rally in Spain

women of the antifascist resistance in near Castelluccio, Italy

various ways to support the National Liberation Movement. It has been calculated that approximately twenty-five thousand women died in battle, and some two thousand women attained officer's rank."

Petronella Lee gives us quick overall scans of the many roles of women in these antifascist wars, along with striking examples. There's Salaria Kea, the only Black woman in the volunteer Abraham Lincoln Brigade of Americans in the Spanish Civil War. Who was at first fundraising for Ethiopian hospitals which were being bombed by Mussolini's air force. But when she was rejected for enlistment by the Ethiopian army, switched her activity to a closer antifascist military that would accept her. Women were liberating themselves by any means necessary in fighting fascism. Because there's no sense in fighting for freedom in general if you don't free yourself along the way. Actually, it is the only way that it works.

In addition to being soldiers and intelligence agents, of course, women were assassins for real. Alongside being medical workers and couriers. Prison breaks were organized by them. While false identity papers were crafted by them. Women formed midnight sabotage teams to blow up telephone lines and power transmissions. And so on, as far as the imagination can reach. But that only taps the surface of what women's antifascism reshaped the communities around them to reflect. Contrary to macho stereotypes. Which restrict women in war to being victims. At best lesser helpers of "real" fighters, who are young able-bodied male soldiers. Most often dismissed as passive onlookers waiting on the sidelines for male help to arrive.

Petronella Lee emphasizes that these past stories can't be just "inspirational" romanticized examples to us. As the macho left so often does in abstracting us away from our real lives. These difficult, brave, creative women fighting against fascism also grew critical lessons for us. Things all antifascists and everyone fighting for human liberation have to stop and think about.

She draws a whole list of lessons for us to think about. "First, conceptualize anti-fascist resistance broadly and engage in multi-layered struggle. Embrace a variety of organizing strategies and tactics, and move away from the tendency to look at anti-fascist struggle in terms of a hierarchical ranking in which certain forms of struggle (e.g. combat/ fighting, involvement in formal political organizations, etc.) are placed at the top, and all other forms of struggle are seen as secondary and less important. Anti-fascist resistance isn't just one thing. It involves a lot of different types of activities, and requires a diversity of things."

Antifascists have to find the situation that uses their skills. You have to conceptualize yourself as a weapon against fascism. And develop your strengths. Develop the political situation that weapon works in.

She reminds us that antifascist struggle for us can't ever be separate from feminism. Women organizing women to strike blows absolutely is feminism. Same with political education, labor organizing, creating women's autonomous power underneath the surface of community life, and onward.

All this is developed in a more detailed texture in this zine. Petronella Lee manages to give us an overview of the classic antifascist women's activism in only eight pages. So easy to read that there's no sense in my going on about it. Hope you have just checked it out yourself. Her conclusions, what she finds in all this women's story, are invaluable.

i noticed that there are both pluses and minuses about her working the story of women fighting fascism this way. With these kind of historic capitalist wartime examples. The positive is that we get to see so many diverse details in a big picture. Women fighting fascism in the widest possible span of roles and battles. Which is encouraging to know we did all this. And can do it again.

But the big drawback is that those old classic battles against fascism are not at all like our own 21st century vibe. That previous 20th century his-story was capitalist nation state wars. Mostly against foreign fascist invaders and occupiers. Like Ethiopians uniting against Italian fascists. Or Yugoslav partisans against the German fascist occupation. But here it's completely different. We white Americans have historically been the invaders and occupiers, for one big stumbling block.

So don't call 911 and expect them to do much for you. Is more the general idea we should have in our minds about fighting this new white fascism. Our own patriarchal capitalist state is much more likely to covertly aid the fascists *against* us. While pretending not to. Which they seem to be doing exactly that right now.

This leads into the one problem i have with *Anti-Fascism Against Machismo*. Though the zine was sparked off by her understanding that this is not our grandparents' fascism. Especially for women. Yet and again, think this zine assumes too much that fighting fascism is only one important but "limited" issue. That will soon go away. That kind of assumption has been common, but pretty much unexamined. Here's my questions and crazy thoughts, anyway (i find getting unpleasantly old, that crazy thoughts seem more and more reasonable).

Click near the end. Where the *Anti-Fascism Against Machismo* zine says: "*Moving to the final point, the last insight is to connect anti-fascism with more ambitious revolutionary goals. Anti-fascism in and of itself is a necessarily limited struggle. It is a reactive and defensive movement that while incredibly important, is much more of a jumping-off point than a desired end-destination.*"

Petronella Lee's project of taking apart and remaking macho *anti-fa* has far reaching implications for women. i think it's remaking hasn't yet reached some questionable root assumptions we've unthinkingly inherited. Such as the belief that fascism is only a shockingly unusual political happening. A bubble in the stream. Which even under evil patriarchal capitalism shouldn't exist. That with the united effort of good people quickly can be slapped away. Returning Western society and our lives to the "normal" capitalism of imperialism's center. Which feels so much safer and more familiar to white women. That's what is widely assumed. As part of the invisible atmosphere of capitalist ideological thought control if nothing else. Yet and again, i don't think that easy assumption is true.

Fascism doesn't come as an out of place barbaric leftover from some old dark age. How can it? Since it wasn't born in any ancient time at all. It was first born in the 1920s major industrial class wars. Right in the heart of 20th century Western Europe. *Fascism comes from the capitalist future.* It isn't going away now. Not as long as advanced patriarchal capitalism is the society. Because that's what has been strongly generating it all along.

Advanced capitalism is uncaringly trampling over its own built-up civilization. Abandoning its own birth society as it keeps changing shape towards something even more gigantic. Whether you can explain it all or not, no one can deny that is what we are witnessing. Those things as they were don't mean anything now. The traditional mainstream economics and politics of even the late "Superpower" 20th century no longer work. Figures such as Bill Clinton and George Bush are like old unemployed tv game show hosts. i see them signing autographs at the local supermarket opening.

Patriarchal capitalism now inexorably pushes societies towards both extremes. It's the populist right against varieties of radical anticapitalism. That both Trump and Bernie leapt out of the men's room into unexpected mass fandom in 2016 is typical. We struggled with mass white support for right-wing agendas. Like packing the capitalist fake courts over women's rights to abortion and other issues of our own bodies. To consign our bodies, our lives back to the control of the patriarchal state. On the other end, thousands of white women came spontaneously to join a large diversity of peoples to camp and protest the Dakota Access Pipeline, by the Standing Rock Sioux reservation. Indigenous women and youth were an example, playing a large initiating and leadership role in that fight.

The growth in political energy worldwide has shifted, first most visibly to the far right. Now always including fascists and genocidal men of all unsavory kinds. The other trend reborn out of this neocolonial world system, is a new anti-capitalist left at the other extreme. Which is centered on the always precarious rising of oppressed women against the fortifications of capitalist patriarchy. Like the escaped shafts of anger that made obscure "Ferguson" also world famous. And gave Black lesbian community workers a chance to quietly shape different kinds of Black politics. Away from the stale leftovers of 1960s daze. Politics based right or wrong on their own queer political witness.

So i think that an *antifa* that sees itself as a "necessarily limited struggle" might not be so relevant at the moving struggle's edge. A "limited" antifascism can't ever return us to some previous safer same place anyway. Because that's being swept away by waves larger than any of us. That's why everything is so uncertain for everyone now.

i've been writing this to help keep the discussion going. To point women towards Petronella Lee's advance in our political understanding. And to make what contribution i can, far away now from the battlefield. If i can suggest anything useful at all, it would be to move women's whole tumult and outrage and resistance into a larger political picture. By which i don't mean something philosophical or more intellectual.

We know the Big Pink Blob doing a hostile takeover of the white man's capitol was a kind of long-shot political accident. And inevitable at the same time. As a soldier stepping on a landmine in a war zone is a kind of long-shot accident and inevitable. In that there's no innocent parties involved. Because right now the acting white majority is fighting dirty for their lives in a certain way. For every advantage and edge their families and communities ever had. And they know it. It's war zone time and they subconsciously want it that way. That's why white fascism has suddenly become much more relevant for more of them, if on the edge of their vision.

What we're all fighting over is really simple — the end of men's white race. The end of folk's whiteness as an very artifically constructed but ruling identity on the ground. Along with their "great" nation-empire. All into the big swirling garbage disposal drain of modern history. Not going to argue here all the pros and cons. Not all the long history and race talk.

Whiteness is just one of the most unnatural inventions in human his-story. Though we believe in it devoutly. Like it was some man's religious cult with its captive women. i mean out-of-the-world strange. Once in Europe there was no whiteness for many, many centuries. The accepted idea of "race" as we know it and live it out every day, didn't exist. Feudal and early capitalist men crudely assumed that different European nationalities were different biological beings. Nations were races, in effect. So criminal laws and judges in Anglo-Saxon London ruled that way. Down by law, in the 1600s and 1700s, those courts said that the Welsh and Irish were by nationality naturally subhuman. Biologically inclined to crime. As such they could be found guilty of a crime by their origins alone. Though their faces might be white as a bleeding out body.

Do you know what really vexed Adolf when he and his merry men took state power in 1933 Germany? That his fascist bureaucrats didn't know how to draft racial laws. Because no examples of race laws had ever been done anywhere in Europe, ever. So happy Adolf instructed his men to purchase copies of the American laws on race to imitate. Since it had turned out that America was not only the wealthiest, most technologically advanced capitalist power in the world. But also the leader of fake whiteness thinking. Adolf pointed out how America's very foundation wasn't nationality or religion or even politics, but race. We were the very first nation to enact sweeping racial laws and always make race a major legal distinction in everything from politics and commerce to the bedroom.

For America to even exist, inventing whiteness was a necessity. Because America isn't a geography. It's more a corporate brand. Whiteness defined and uniformed their imported mass social army. Needed to invade, genocide up, repopulate, and garrison an entire large continent. The richest prize ever in the world his-story of capitalism. But this is in greater than ever crossfire now. Since whiteness is objectively becoming as much a drag as it is an opportunity. Even to their society. 50/50 i'd say as a guess. Think the ruling class is having the same opinion about it.

For centuries, whites liked the u.s.a. As long as they stayed on top as the euro-settler garrison of empire over everyone else. Now they are freaking out. Reconsidering their loyalties. Notice how all of a sudden, Canada, Australia and New Zealand are envied as better places to live by so many whites? The acting white majority is doubling down because their entire world is threatened. Our fake specialness and made-up ethnic exclusivity is crumbling. Whiteness is running out.

As the neocolonial stage of the world capitalist system more and more jumbles multicultural populations carelessly.

Neocolonialism as a radical political term simply means "colonialism of a new kind". It still is colonialism, the domination and forced occupation of one people by another. Example: as in the euro-colonialism leading up to the 20th century. As when a small British military and commercial invasion force numbering only in the thousands was represented at first by the private East India Company. Starting in the 19th century they gradually conquered and welded together the many small principalities and states and tribes of the Indian subcontinent. Into one giant inorganic Indian colonial state. It was like a rat owning an elephant. The "British Raj" repressed matriarchies and imposed capitalist patriarchal laws and exclusions, robbing Indian women of roles and rights. In imitation of what euro-capitalism had done to first get all charged up at home. Millions of Indians died back then in manufactured capitalist famines. As even basic foodstocks were shipped all the way from India back to Europe.

Western imperialism later had to reshape itself into a more sophisticated neocolonialism. Giving way to guerrilla anti-colonial revolutions sweeping the globe by the mid-20th century. Neocolonialism where it pretended to honor the political independence of former colonial nations and peoples of the capitalist periphery. But kept indirectly feeding on them behind the scenes. Still parasitically extracting large profits from unequal trade and strategic mineral extraction. Working through bribed native political leaders, military dictatorships, and dependent local capitalist classes. Western patriarchal capitalism always encourages the most backward cultural and political currents. To keep native peoples off compass and off balance. There is much more to what neocolonialism is and how it works, but this is a barest description to start off from.

Growing up i never thought there wouldn't be a White America. Whites filled to the horizon whether big city or farming country. And every niche from business managers to soldiers, postal letter carriers to city bus drivers. Now it's been years since i've even seen a white letter carrier around. On my busy city bus line (not that i can physically get on it anymore) a white bus driver might appear only once every month or so, i hear.

When i talk about the fight over capitalist patriarchy's compulsion to own us, i keep referring to women's actual bodies. As the material terrain being fought over. i am doing this deliberately. To rudely and crudely remind women that this isn't just a battle over someone's nice or bad ideas.

All human liberation or oppression must be realized in the actual material world. That is, on who has what space or territory or terrain or physical manifestation. A people who do not possess any territory in the material world, often do not even get to own their own bodies. We are real proof of that, as women as the first euro-capitalist colony should know. From centuries of experience of not owning even a space as small as our own bodies.

White women are angered at the patriarchal capitalist assumption that men can leave us without territory physical or social. That our bodies, our lives should have no autonomy of our own. Yet, Indigenous peoples point out that euro-settler genocide capitalism denies them any right to so much as an inch of land. Permanently theirs for their culture and self-determination to manifest itself. Many of us don't want to understand that.

We know this since patriarchal capitalism doesn't even bother to hide the fact. Any time they want Indigenous land. For petrofuel pipelines or mines or highways or waste sites or real estate developments. They simply take it. Ever so legally or not. By casual force. For nothing Native peoples have or Black people have can be permanently, safely theirs for their community and self-determination. In an entire continent of thousands of miles, not one inch.

The 1960s feminist awakening talked about women needing our own material territory. Our "space". Whether it was Ginny Woolf's "a room of one's own" or a college department of our own. Or lesbian land or the "Michigan" festival. How is this different at the root from what Rez traditionals or Black nationalists build?

What's basic for us is that without white women and our repro-ductive labor there is no white race. Much less any whitest nation. Which is why not only the fascists, but the whole acting white majority can't stop fighting. To recapture our bodies. Can't stop needing to own women as their most critical national resource. The attack on us isn't going away, maybe not in your lifetime. But don't we already know that instinctively by now? We're in it for a long war.

Patriarchal socialism has always falsely emphasized how mod-ern society was built on mostly male industrial labor. Sixties radical feminism replied that the most basic labor in all economic production is *reproduction*. Their primal insight was that women's unwaged labor in reproducing society's workers was and is the most essential produc-tion. **They named women as a gender-class being the first proletariat, the first conquered colony. And eventually the last.**

In their own ways, the broader white right understands this very well. Better than we do, i sometimes think. That's why their litmus test for joining their larger right has become abortion (which of course, only

Aryan Nations supporters join skinheads and Klansmen at a Pulaski, Tennessee rally, October 7, 1989. (credit: Center for Democratic Renewal)

dishonestly fronts for the war of who owns women's bodies). Just our very partial, limited escape in the 1960s onward shook White America to its foundations. Once women can have independent personal lives, jobs and education, we stop being willing to be forced into being house bound, large-scale reproducers of someone else's necessary labor power and foot soldiers. Birth rates plummet. Big majority populations shrink and shrink. As they should. For the survival of human beings on this planet.

That's why they're picketing Planned Parenthood most every day of the week. Rain and cold. That's why they hate abortion doctors far more than the most famous male socialists and anarchists. That's why the white right can't just "let it go" with us. As another win-some-lose-some political issue. Why they can't compromise on not permitting women's human rights. They have to own us and our bodies. Or lose everything they've always been as a people. Without owning women there is no whitest nation-empire. They're driven by the nightmare of falling into being a subject minority in now someone else's nation.

It's that simple. That's why white fascism here and now isn't a "limited" issue that will easily pass away. Thinking of white fascism in isolation is misleading. They only exist now as an acid thread sheltered within the flow of a much larger white far right. That has a known u.s. following in the millions. A relatively large white far right with diverse faces and views, but with common catchy populist themes. Taking as primary the scapegoating of the "other". Misogyny expressed in hatred

of feminism. Pseudo-genetic politics that has made them a self-proclaimed special people. While reviving the legacy of "patriotic" wars and the right to commemorate their human rights crimes. White fascists there are already part of the loose militias and terrorist fringes that are the forward edge of the offensive.

So there's a mass populist shift towards a reanimated white right empire. It could be here longer than most *antifa* are thinking. For a tip, we could ask the Indigenous peoples how long those euro-settler home invaders are likely to stay on uninvited in their living rooms? Right now the new populist right can represent close to a majority of the white communities of this euro-settler empire. And tomorrow is uncertain.

Moreover. As when radical white women think about fighting fascism, aren't we unconsciously picturing us confronting only small groups of *men*? Emphasis on the word "men". i notice that even Petronella Lee only gives examples of women fighting fascist men. But are you or i ready to deal with many white women shouting hate at us? Stepping forward to drive us out of their white neighborhoods and

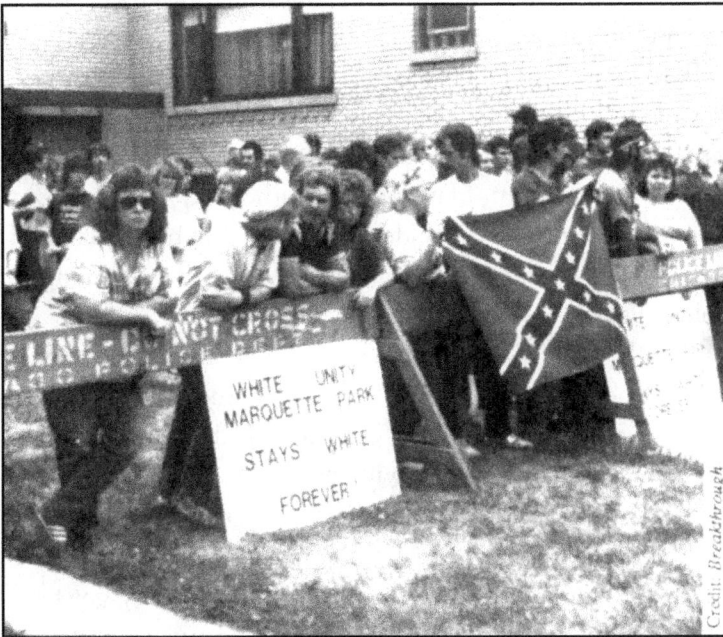

Credit: *Breakthrough*

schools and jobs? Been there, done that, girl, and it was surreal but it sure wasn't pleasant.

Do we acknowledge the strategic political-military reality that many white women may not be with us fighting the white right? It's important that we understand why white women more than anybody are so split politically right now. Want to repeat that.

There's a modern capitalist propaganda of women as "naturally" peaceful and affirming of everyone. That's just another typecast Disney cartoon. Our real world is much more gritty and dialectical materialist than that, so obviously. When i say that women were the first colony, that's more than a literary metaphor. 1960s radical feminist scholars in Europe did research going back to their foremothers' story in the Witchhunt starting in the 13th century. What they found was evidence that massive internal repression and expropriation of successful women in the late Middle Ages produced extra economic surpluses. For the growing of more aggressive men's states. That later became patriarchal capitalist nations. Then in later centuries, special added exploitation of women in the colonial systems of the Global South, such as in Bermuda, Africa and India, helped jump-start European industrialization.

That women under the beginnings of euro-capitalism were that first systemic colony, still reverberates to this day in us. Many white women don't realize this, because they grew up under the more indirect *neo*-colonialism. Have never breathed any other air. But my life like that of so many other older women, bridges both periods of the trailing away of old women's colonialism. And then the coming newer neocolonialism.

i was born in New Jersey because my moms escaped her childhood home herself in Minnesota. My grandmother was an escapee, too, as a young woman from Czarist Russian in the bad old daze. My only family inheritance seems to be a willingness to escape. Very precious for a free woman, i feel.

When grandmom got to London as a safe pausing place from pogroms and deportations, a Jewish refugee aid society got her ship passage to South Africa. Where as a breeding woman she would be wanted to build up the Jewish community in Britain's new white South African colony. But she didn't like the looks of that, so it was on to another boat. With the refugee husband she had joined forces with along the way. The other alternative was ship passage and on to a place in the u.s. Midwest they'd never even heard of. There isolated in Wisconsin, the Jewish refugee society hoped to establish some kind of alternative co-op type circle of Jewish family farmers. To honorably wipe away the antisemitic stereotype of Jews as only big city cheating money lenders and merchants.

Well, the Jewish fantasy farms didn't work, as you probably expected. So speaking no English, my grandparents fell back on more familiar slums in Minnesota. There he died when my moms was seven. So her own mom and her eked out a survival livelihood working for a small neighborhood grocery store. My moms as a child had to come to the shop after school. Translating for her mom who didn't speak English. Helping her mom by pulling the little handcart carrying customer's bags of groceries to their homes.

She wanted to escape that grim life, too, as so many millions of women bottomfish everywhere do. But in the normal course of things women were socially imprisoned. As a colonized people. Held below, most education, professions, businesses, trades, and government employment. In other words, segregated below most of the main capitalist economy. To keep them focused on involuntarily providing sex and labor reproduction on a mass scale. The two regular jobs that respectable women could have back then that earned them enough to have "a room of their own" were schoolteacher and telephone operator. No wonder most women were under pressure to find a husband and his paycheck. In return for sex and children. Oh, it was the Depression outside the door, then, too.

Then an important thing intersected her life with a bang. The Big Bang Theory in real life was imperialism acting as antifascist in World War II. Which blew the economy upside down on its greedy head. No more time for Mr. Depression. Instead more and more factories turning out tanks and crude pine barracks furniture and boots and army office

forms and trucks and canned rations and everything. Like the opening of an alternative universe. Suddenly there were all kinds of "men's
jobs" for millions of women in basic industry. The celebrated "Rosie the
Riveter" thing.

Moms escaped poverty after school even better by leaving for
Washington, D.C. Which had become White America's newest boom
town. A glittering Las Vegas of the state bureaucracy. Where many
thousands of adventuresome young single white women had migrated
from all over to fill the new office jobs. In all the expanding bureaucra-
cies of a "greatest" state. Which was conducting the "greatest" world war
ever.

World imperialist war cost too-large-to-be-exactly-counted
deaths of tens and tens of millions of women, children and men. The
bombing out of major cities. A-bombs leapfrogging miles of aerial fire-
bombings. To say nothing of the Holocaust and countless other mass
civilian slayings by all sides as collateral damage. In odd contradiction,
my Moms and her single white women coworkers experienced all this
carnival of horror on their end as a happy time. Real jobs, classy u.s.
government person status, real paychecks in no war zone at all except
ducking incoming dicks. White women's rooming houses where going
out after 5 to bars every night, to socialize with young men was perfectly okay. No patriarchal family in sight. It was a breakthrough for
her personally.

With backwards and forwards for white women inching into the
1950s and then 1960s. Open male supremacy and contempt for women
was still the normal. As late as 1957, as u.s. Labor Secretary Robert
Reich has commented: "United Airlines proudly announced that its
'executive service' between New York and Chicago featured comfortable slippers, a steak dinner, and 'no woman on board except for two
stewardesses.'"[5]

Yet and again, white women were getting some small share in "our"
u.s. empire becoming the dominant world industrial-military power.
Being loyal to whiteness and thus empire was rock bottom settler-col-
onial politics for us. Just as it has always been in taking over the whole

Indigenous continent and keeping confined the rebellious New Afrikan internal colony.

No criticism at all of Moms, but here we can trace a continuing divergence between white euro-settler life here and what the heck was going on in the rest of the world. That we were sure enough taking over. Seems the worse for them, the better for us. Maybe take that as a vague rule of thumb. She even found a good European emigrant husband. They moved to Whitesville. My sisters and i popped out of the toaster oven, start of home movie again.

Did this little upwardly mobile story mean that any white women's colonization had been left behind? Not exactly. Remember none of this was "natural" or spontaneous or unplanned. What happened to women was all done as conscious social engineering by capitalists and state agencies. That's why it's called the patriarchy.

When i escaped to start my queer straight trans whatever life at age 17, the world for white women was not what it is now. While obviously change of some kind was happening. More kinds of jobs and education were gradually opening up to white women. Not that i was noticing. It was common for banks to refuse new accounts to single women without a man to co-sign. Not unusual for bars and "better restaurants" to turn away single women. See, we might be prostitutes.

It was brought to me that my sexual experimenting equals i'd better get birth control. Going to Planned Parenthood meant learning a little dancing. The law said they couldn't give us birth control without a husband's consent. No husband, no birth control. Taking advantage of a loophole, i was guided to say my "fiancé" who was temporarily out of town due to family illness, was giving his eager consent in advance. Back then, even Trojans and Sheiks at the drugstore were held out of sight behind the counter. You had to ask the male pharmacist for permission. Asking men for permission was a big feature of women's life then. Yet and again, i could make a simple living and roam the streets at night. Looking to make trouble. What more could a girl ask?

As the 1960s started bigger change hung in the air. As before in u.s. empire her-story, the advance of Black struggle would persuade white women to venture forth and make our own movement again. But the breakout of the women's liberation movement and feminism was surprising at every corner. Didn't play out like it was expected. The cultural change and wham-bam battles were tremendous. Modern technology played a role as it does right now. Having "the pill" was big like being given machine guns or something. You could be using birth control and no man would even know or have a say. i loved that the Church and the rightwing hated it and were powerless to stop it. (note: Big pharma has more muscle under capitalism than big church).

Seemed like every day women were invading somewhere they had been kept out of. One of my dreams when i was a young girl was to be a tug boat captain. Bringing ocean liners and freighters with the waves into harbor all day. But in the real girls' world i had been formerly condemned to, i couldn't even wear my pants and tennis shoes to school.

But when my sister and i went to a 1950s girls' summer camp a couple of summers, there it was all reversed. They had archery. Baseball was natural for me. Rowing was fun. The camp even let us shoot a beginner's .22 cal bolt action, single shot rifle. Liked that, too, and hit the target. Yet and again, couldn't do any of that as a life, as a grown up woman then. And women weren't allowed as tug boat crews much less become captains. Came along too early, i guess. But in the patriarchal capitalist system's neocolonial zone shift.

In a women's coincidence that i do believe in, my niece in another place caught the same waterfront dream i had many years later. In the 1980s she talked her way onto a dockside crew for the ferry. For awhile she loved it, and worked hard at it for some time. Carrying heavy loops of rope, accepting work injuries from a physically tough job. But eventually she burned out at the oppression of all the "equal opportunity". Constant sexism. Being given the short end of the stick in work assignments. So that the men's days would be easier. And never ever being allowed to advance jobwise. In this day there are women captains in the many types of boats and ships that work the harbor and rivers and nearby ocean to that city. But always only few of them. Sprinkles on top of the pastry, i always call it.

Speaking of transportation: Understanding women as a neo-colony, is maybe easiest by first thinking of those NASA women's spacesuits. Or rather, that singular, only one woman's spacesuit. This isn't about individual achievement or promotion, at all. That's just the distorted patriarchal capitalist form that our present reality is presented to us as.

Photo Credit: Peg Hunter

In March 2019, NASA was proudly set to send two women astronauts up to spacewalk together for the first time. Then, oops, they had to cancel that publicity rocket. Had to admit that they had forgotten that in their whole space program they only had one spacesuit sized for a woman. After decades of sending astronauts into space, NASA had never thought to have a supply of spacesuits for women astronauts! They only had one that would fit. So Christina Koch went up with a male astronaut and Ann McClain was scrubbed until a suit could be ordered from China or Amazon.

NASA started in the Kennedy era. As a designated superior white men's elite. Not that women weren't there. *We're always there.* In that early barely computer age, they needed an entire department to do all the orbital and physics and aeronautical mathematical calculations to make flight plans. White male mathematicians and physicists willing to do behind the scenes grunt work for low pay were few and far between. So NASA got smart and recruited a secret department of Black women college graduates. Many underemployed mathematicians and scientists. And for many years they worked getting NASA spaceflights on the correct paths. Unknown to the outside world until very recently.

Then, under pressure, NASA began to let sprinkles of women into the training astronaut program. Never intending to let more than a few ever fly in space. Token sprinkles on the Tom of Finland's cake. In 2003 one-third of women astronauts wouldn't fit into any available NASA spacesuits. The size small suits, which most women would use, had been discontinued as not cost effective. Since most NASA astromen wore larger sizes. While 12 of the 38 current astronauts are women, at the start of the year 2019 there were still no size small suits and the only one precious size medium. Clearly the NASA sub-sub-branch of the capitalist patriarchy had simply forgotten about women astronauts needing any spacesuits at all in space. Maybe we were supposed to hold our breath and wear garbage bags? This is after a generation of NASA spaceflights. Where women are allowed to advance and fill minority roles. But only as assistants acting as though they were men within abusive capitalist patriarchal structures. Ah, neocolonialism has that distinctive toxic smell to it?[6]

But this does relate to what happened to the radical women's liberation movement of the 1960s-70s. One night it was burning intensely. Throwing out unheard of insights and travel directions for us. Seemingly the next it all disappeared. The capitalist patriarchy started opening jobs and education and advancement for women. Especially educated women. It was like a California Gold Rush. Lesbians got to come out, and even get married. Set up legally protected nuclear households. Yes, and in the process women got irradiated. As one famous lesbian polemicist said of the women's movement's surprising evaporation: *"Everyone went home to a nuclear relationship and a career."*

Was that progress for women in some form? Needed human rights however unsatisfactory? Of course it was. But the outward form of change can take place in different contexts. Which determine what they really become. In **colonialism**, patriarchal capitalist institutions would be racist and male in makeup, culture and function. Women would be excluded except as voiceless "hands" and "bodies" carrying out lower tasks. In **neocolonialism**, patriarchal capitalist institutions have a publicly positive multicultural identity, smiling at women as consumers and workers. At the same time be constructed as before to racist and male agendas, composition and culture. Women would be officially encouraged but informally tightly controlled. Allowed to reinforce crumbling male hierarchy but without changing it.

In women's liberation, women wouldn't need or be in a white boys tinker-toy NASA. We'd do it ourselves all different from the ground up if we needed it. Same with the whole human economy and society, as far as we're concerned. Under neocolonialism we are temporarily allowed to play roles in and reinforcing patriarchal capitalist institutions. Which like NASA have nothing to do with benefiting any women at all. These two things are not the same.

There's a slice of white women now who are sympathetic to rebellion and change, especially with the Trump game show and the far right threatening. This is a small minority yet. There's a much larger group of white women who only want us to keep going straight ahead. Very straight. Keep gaining ground for ourselves in economics and rights the way they feel we have. And then there's a large group of women who are supporting the white populist right. Who are rallying behind euro-settler colonial domination of society forever. As the primal group loyalty that has always given white women their small share of safety and whatever we have.

It isn't that millions of any white women are into converting to fascism, of course. Yet right now millions of white women are willing to vote for right-wing populism, complete with a nutty fuhrer. Whose hater movement shelters and feeds within it the outright white fascists as they work on. Our clashing with other white women in some real way is inevitable looking forward.

In the bitter Black vs. White civil rights daze, i remember, white women played a strategic if often underestimated role. They took the lead by the many thousands in building massive grassroots campaigns in neighborhoods and entire cities. Time and again mobilizing women's grassroots, door to door, power. Not for us, but against us. *Against the nonviolent civil rights movement.* For the police and klan and white men's power. Remember talking to a white woman who as a teenager had joined the Black sit-ins. She had grown up in a Southern city. In fact a state capital of a Deep South state. When Black students started sitting-in protests against their colonial oppression, she was moved to go downtown and join them. Though the white police made sure that she was physically separated from the beatings and arrests they gave out to try and terrorize the young Black women and men. Impressed that she had braved that much, i asked her how many white women in her city had joined the Black sit-ins for freedom back then? She said, "I was the only one." In an entire city of white women. Does that make our own colonialism less abstract for us?

It was white women more than white men who as always did the dirty household work of keeping schools segregated. Of maintaining the Color White. Of holding together white communities as right-wing social fortresses. Which they now are revealed to be to this day.

Just like that recent PBS documentary on country music showed. Tammy Wynette became a country singing success for white women with her blunt songs about not taking abuse from their men. But she only became a real star with her historic right-wing hit, "Stand By Your Man". Both sides of the record are truly hers. That's our contradiction as a people-class, too.

Here in the metropolis. In the heart of world patriarchal capitalism. The most educated women in the world don't know what to do next. Which we hate to admit.

Yet and again, what the intense but short-lived Sixties radical feminism laid out on the table is true. Why the German radical philosopher Christina Thurmer-Rohr said it just as Malcolm X had for his people.

We have to step off. To leave the dense, encumbering, blood-feeding culture of men's civilization best we can.

White women don't know what to do & can't really know what to do from where we are. We're in the wrong place to answer those questions. We first have to step off and detox from patriarchy. To get our bearings on our own. To set out learning from our own plans. We need to walk away. And start on our own forty years in the wilderness.

Alright. i've sung my song.

Joining the Conversation

Veronica L., July 21, 2020

I finally got a chance to sit down and study both of your texts. I read them both when they first came out, but I hadn't read them both together. I also managed to convince some comrades to talk about them with me. No men invited. We had a good conversation and I feel compelled to share some of my thoughts. It is important to continue having this conversation publicly. Perhaps others will feel drawn to join in.

I will write this mostly in the singular, but obviously the ideas are not all mine. Partly because ideas are never entirely our own, partly because some of these ideas specifically came out of conversations with friends and comrades, but I am writing this text on my own. I'm also not trying to represent everyone's opinions from those conversations. Mostly I'm trying to clarify my own thoughts.

Photo Credit: Peg Hunter

Part I: Fascism, Anti-Fascism, what does it all mean?

First I will address our changing context. I first saw Tammy's text published in May of 2019 and Butch's response in December 2019. I began this response in June 2020, in the midst of a full-blown uprising against the police and for Black liberation in the so-called US, after two months of intense anti-colonial struggle earlier this year that is often referred to as #ShutDownCanada.[1] It was also our third month of the coronavirus pandemic. The city where I live had started the process of deconfinement, though people were and are still dying every day, mostly elderly people and people of colour.

Here in Quebec, the organized anti-fascists (i.e. Montréal Antifasciste) say that 2019 was a pretty quiet year for the far right. This doesn't determine the future, but it is worth noting. So far, 2020 has also been relatively uneventful for them. Despite sections of the far-right movement declining, there remains a high level of far-right power in government. As Montréal Antifasciste put it, "The decline in activity on Québec's far-right doesn't signal a victory for anti-fascist forces. To the contrary, with a majority populist government in the Assemblée Nationale, a government that moved rapidly in its first year in power to pass the racist Bill 21 ('an Act Respecting Laicity') on state secularism, as well as gagging debate to adopt a variety of anti-immigrant measures, it is reasonable to postulate that the right-wing forces are simply taking a breather, because they feel they've achieved some of their main goals."[2]

In the year or two immediately after Trump was elected, anti-fascism became a main way that new people were becoming politicized, even in so-called Canada. The kind of anti-fascism that was animating those political changes in people then isn't so much at the forefront now. These days, people are being politicized through participation and as witnesses to the movement for Black liberation and struggles against the police. People of the far right attack these protests (or sometimes participate in them), but, in the most publicized places, these far-right elements are not a main focus of the fight.[3] This shift in context animates how I'm thinking about this conversation around what fascism and anti-fascism mean.

Butch's text raises the question, *where do we take our definition of anti-fascism from?* This reads as a spin off of *who defines anti-fascism?* For Butch, it is the original Black Panther Party (BPP). I get the sense that for Tammy, it is the BPP and also the Anti-Racist Action networks from the 90s—the punks and skinheads who were beating up Nazis across the US and Canada. It is from this history that we see a more specific definition of anti-fascism take hold. It is at least the recognition of certain tactics that we have seen dominate the popular understanding of anti-fascism in the last 5 years—beating up Nazis, "no platforming" (i.e., getting events and other publicly visible events featuring the far right and their cronies canceled), doxxing, and counter-protests. Butch takes issue with this way of defining anti-fascism. She has a point; when we understand anti-fascism by strictly these tactics, we change how we approach the fight. The tactics will inform who we target more than any other factor, which then limits the struggle itself. Both Butch and Tammy argue this in different ways.

Tammy calls for a distinction between various far-right groups and actors so that we may pose different strategies for dealing with each of them, but the need is also more grave than that. However, this is an undeniably useful call, given the past five years of street fights between the far right and anti-fascists at demonstrations that have preceded our current situation. The rebellion that has arisen in the wake of George Floyd's murder has involved a wide range of tactics, from burning down a police precinct to widespread looting to large day-time demonstrations in hundreds of cities to negotiations with city councils and school boards. There is obviously a lot of disagreement about tactics happening within the movement; the disagreement I am most interested in here is about white people participating in and, at times, "instigating" riots. This conversation is being undeniably influenced by the four years of spectacular physical violence between anti-fascists and fascists in the streets of the so-called US.

In the first few weeks of the uprising, there were unprecedented occurrences of white people calling on each other to "shut down" white rioters who are "instigating" (see screenshots below). This has led to instances of white people beating up other white people during demonstrations,[4] which is new to me, as well as white people being handed over to the police in demos,[5] which is not new. I attribute this first phenomenon in part to the normalization of the spectacle of anti-fascists beating up Nazis in the streets over the past four years. This in addition to a glaring and unanswered question that we have inherited from movements past – *what role do white people have to play in an anti-racist struggle?* This larger question is intimately related to questions about distinguishing between various far-right groups and actors. Nevertheless, it does seem like Tammy and Butch are using different understandings of anti-fascism in order to achieve different ends. And both those definitions are useful if we are to fully understand what we're up against.

If that's anti-fascism, then what is fascism? Central question here. One that Butch presses Tammy on, asking us to push back against "the belief that fascism is only a shockingly unusual political happening." (97) On the surface, I don't think Tammy would disagree and neither do I. I see the use of being clear about the overlap between fascism and white supremacy. I even see the rhetorical strategy of using this word to describe the normal state of things under anti-Black, settler colonial, patriarchal, and capitalist realities on this continent. But Tammy's instincts of wanting to distinguish between different kinds

If you're a white person at these protests, and you see other white people starting shit like throwing rocks or starting fires, you need to shut that down. That's not solidarity, it's agitation, and the ones who will wind up paying for it are Black and brown people

10:27 AM · May 30, 2020

48.9K Retweets **599** Quote Tweets **154.3K** Likes

Replying to

THIS⬆ As a white ally it is out job to support and help amplify the message, not to take over. If white people are inciting violence or elevating tensions they need to be checked, fast, and removed if they don't immediately back down. Our privilege endangers lives.

of fascism is helpful, if only to figure out our specific strategies against variant parts of the far-right movement and then expand this to include different strategies against the liberal power structure that is always related to fascism in our context.

White supremacists and the state itself share many goals and some tactics. The most basic interaction of the two, seen when the state plays cheerleader to white supremacist mobs (or when the police literally help far-right groups avoid arrest), helps us to think about the ways in which these tactics and roles shift over time. Rather than treating Butch and Tammy's views of fascism as competing definitions, we can hold both an analysis of fascism developed at a time when the state and far right were basically indistinguishable (as Butch does), and another at a moment when the state was taking care to distance itself from the "fringe" (as Tammy does). This is useful in thinking through these interconnections, and the accompanying broadening of tactics Tammy is calling for.

It makes sense that Tammy swings back and forth between identifying the bedrock of so-called US and Canadian democracy as fascism and also calling it white supremacy. Even as she wants to take it all down. This is why parts of her text could apply to anarchism as a movement just as easily as anti-fascism. Except that in this moment, anti-fascism is much more generalized as a sentiment than anarchism (specifically because anti-fascist ideas are widely understood to be less revolutionary). Anti-fascism could be seen as a gateway to more radical politics, or at least it seemed to be working that way from 2016–2019. Hard to tell now.

So fascism and the founding white supremacist principles of the US and Canada are interrelated. One way of thinking about this is that fascists regularly pave the way for liberals to march after them, fascism pushes the boundaries that liberalism can then fill in, and the threat of fascism is used by the state and liberals to maintain power. Therefore, fascism is related to but not the same thing as white supremacy.

There is a tendency in our political circles to say "everything is fascist," but because anti-fascism has a specific set of tactics associated

Members of far-right three-percenters posing with police in Olympia, WA in 2020.

with it (which Tammy is trying to expand) that claim doesn't help to develop adequate strategies against fascists. If our movements expand the set of pointed actions and strategies used to fight fascism, this could also create a more nuanced understanding of fascism. Our tactics could then grow beyond the parameters set for us by our enemies.

The current George Floyd Uprising is figuring out how to get people involved in a widening range of ways. Mutual Aid food assistance and deliveries have flourished during the pandemic, with participants picking up food for their neighbors and other vulnerable people. These types of collaborations have translated easily into leaving out water and supplies for the people in the streets, with obvious nods to the lessons from Hong Kong on the front-liners' need for support from the back and vice versa. I heard a story about how the Winnipeg general strike in 1919 was fueled by a year of mutual aid organizing during the Spanish flu epidemic. It makes sense that uprisings come on the heels (or in the midst) of pandemics. Mutual aid and militant tactics can and should fit together. Our movements need all of it.

Part II: The Role of White Women in the Struggle to End Patriarchy, White Supremacy, and Capitalism

A main point Butch makes in her response to Tammy is that white women have an important role to play in ending "men's white race." Though we often think of neocolonialism as only applying to struggles that were explicitly seen as national liberation struggles, Butch says that neocolonialism has also affected the struggles of white women, that it has also coopted white women's struggles by creating a situation "where women are allowed to advance and fill minority roles, but only as assistants acting as though they were men within abusive capitalist patriarchal structures." She says later that women (unclear if she means explicitly white) were the first proletariat and will eventually be the last. Finally, she writes, "what's basic for us is that without white women and our reproductive labor, there is no white race."

What does all that mean? Many parts of the women's liberation movement have been thoroughly coopted since the 1980s, by academia and the non-profit industrial complex. They were undermined by the white upper-middle-class character of their base, which allowed the goals of the movement to morph into a small percentage of white women gaining access to power in white men's world. Power structures shifted marginally to allow some token white women into positions of power, but the basic structure of things stayed the same. Butch makes clear that white women refusing to help white men reproduce the white race would effectively end the white race.

There is a tension here between different ways of understanding whiteness, which Butch sort of acknowledges in her piece. On the one hand, whiteness is something that isn't real. It is a power structure that shifts and changes over time. It isn't biologically set in stone. It is socially produced for specific ends. In this sense, there are some blurry edges to whiteness that make it confusing at times. Whiteness can become somewhat expandable depending on the context. On the other hand, whiteness is very material. It is a material thing that literally needs to be reproduced through the creation of white babies and the reproduction of its institutions (among them the nuclear family and marriage).

In *The Military Strategy of Women and Children*, Butch writes that "revolutionary women's culture begins when we leave the table." Certainly, leaving the table is a big project. Written this way, it becomes clear that the proposal at hand is a revolutionary proposition, not just an individual action. Some white women have been refusing to do reproductive labour for a long time now and this has meant that women of colour have been forced to do it (think surrogacy, wet nurses, live-in caregiver programs, etc.). We must aim for bigger and more strategic ends that are more clear through their means. No more fighting for a seat at the table. More energy spent destroying the table entirely.

How do we leave the table? And who *are we* while we're doing it? In the past, people have called for a revolutionary organization of white women. Butch calls for this implicitly. Amber Hollibaugh talks about lesbian separatism as a form of nationalism, which I hadn't heard before, but it makes a lot of sense.[6] The national liberation struggles of the 60s, 70s, and 80s have always resonated with me as the most recent high point of revolutionary struggle in this context, and there is something super compelling about trying to recreate that high. But the reality of neocolonialism means we can't just rinse and repeat. It won't work.

One form of leaving the table in our present era has been called autonomous organizing. The LIES collective has published the most helpful framing of this conversation that I've seen to date. In their piece on autonomous organizing in *LIES II*, they call for "a practice of autonomy built around the exclusion of cis men, rather than around a static notion of 'womanhood', a gender-essentialist and cis-supremacist notion of 'female-bodied-ness', or an insufficient and problematic notion of 'lesbian separatism.'"[7] They write, "So many of our current projects after all began as a kind of naming: some people getting together, finding a shared circumstance, and then finding a shared interest in approaching it with antagonism, as a start."[8] First, don't assume shared identities, find shared circumstances. Second, approach with antagonism, which I understand to tie in to things Tammy had to say about militancy.

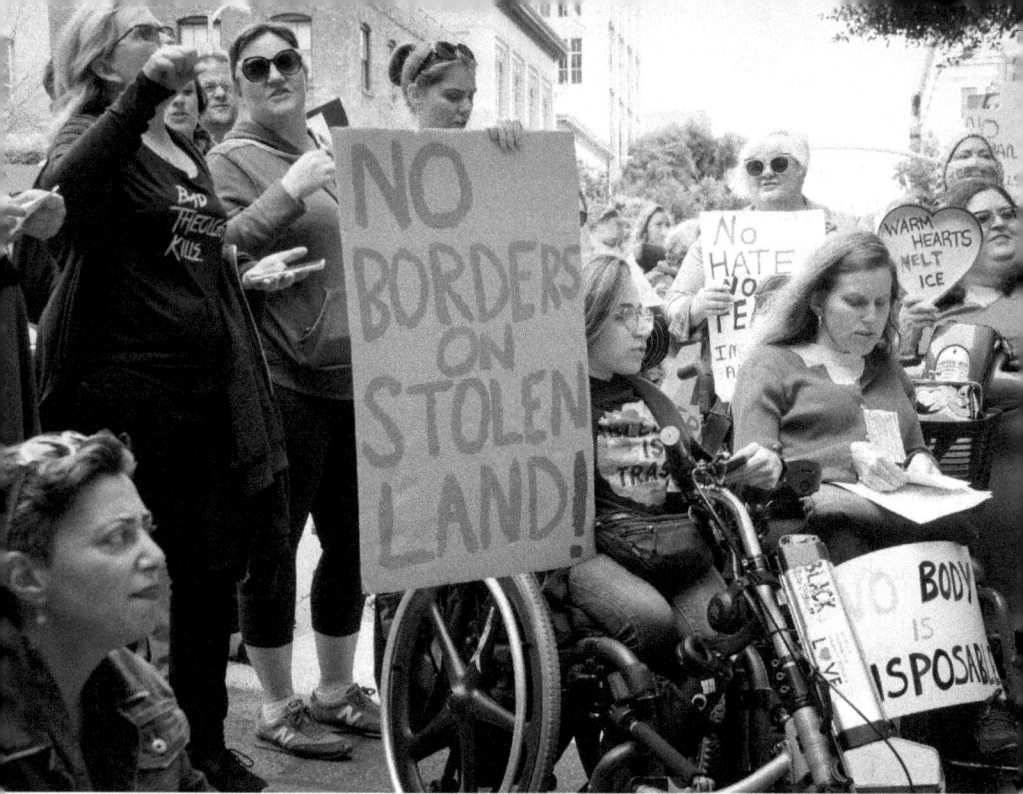

This perspective focuses simply on the exclusion of cis-men, which I understand as an explicit nod to trans and queer liberation movements that have pointed out the gender binary as an institution to destroy alongside patriarchy. In some ways, this articulation of who we are has a tension embedded within it that is similar to the tension I named earlier around whiteness. Gender is at once a socially constructed category that shifts and changes over time, while also being materially concerned with our bodies themselves, how we understand them, and are understood by others, which all can have real material impacts on people's lives. Obviously, there will be tensions and contradictions within formations that do not include cis men, but defining who is in the room in this expansive way can produce useful collaborations across difference while bringing together those who are likely to be able to find shared antagonisms.

However, the most successful moments of autonomous organizing without men that I have tried have also built upon shared politics and affinity. These formations have used autonomous organizing without cis men to strategize the end of white supremacy, of patriarchy, of capitalism, of the settler state. They have de-centered the men who were the glue between different parts of any given political landscape. These spaces with no men became ways for us to build relationships that didn't involve those men, allowing us to carry those relationships over into other organizing projects in our lives. We have cut out the literal middle men in order to give them less power. That is a step towards leaving the table.

Though I want more. I am thinking of the importance of having other reference points or movements to be in conversation with. We aim to be embedded within a constellation of revolutionary movements and groupings as one node within that. We need other movements and spaces to keep us responsible and accountable. Is that happening today? Sort of? Feels closer today than ever before in my life. But the autonomous organizing without cis men in my context has not managed to carve out enough space to hold its own.

What is missing? Why hasn't this happened more? Do people lack the determination to do it? The willingness to take the risks associated with it? A lack of answers (and perhaps, disagreements) to questions around what kind of formation is up for the task? Enough clarity around what it is that we are even trying to do in the broader sense? Probably all of the above.

One block that comes up in relation to Butch's text specifically is about land and the material ability to carve out autonomous space. Butch wrote "The 1960s feminist awakening talked about women needing our own material territory. Our 'space.' Whether it was Ginny Woolf's 'a room of one's own' or a college department of our own. Or lesbian land or the 'Michigan' festival. How is this different at the root from what Rez traditionals or Black nationalists build?" It seems like she's asking this question rhetorically, but I want to find some answers. How is it different for autonomous organizing that excludes men to "need our own material territory"? Does that mean having a land base? Does that mean owning land? If that organizing is mostly made up of white women,[9] what are the implications of that in an anti-Black settler state that has from its beginning involved white women enforcing its hierarchies and advancing its settlement?

We have to seriously think about this question around land and space. Given the history of much of the so-called US and Canada, there are ways of white people relating to land that are thoroughly colonial: buying it, inheriting it, relating to it as property ... even squatting isn't inherently anti-colonial in this context, given the history of white people squatting Native land here. There are ways that relating to land is totally contextual on social position; i.e., the Provisional Government of the Republic of New Africa's relationship to what is now the Southeastern US has liberatory potential in ways that Cascadia doesn't. I am also thinking here about Indigenous sovereignty, as well as the basic idea of land as relation that I understand to come out of Indigenous movements and cultures. There is the reality that this is a conversation to be had between movements and one of the movements in the conversation doesn't exist. Indigenous movements and Black liberation movements are seeing a resurgence today, so we can see what's missing. #MeToo isn't cutting it.[10]

How do we bring it into being? How do we build a movement without men that is committed to an expansive understanding of anti-fascism and that embraces feminist militancy? How do we do that while avoiding the missteps of the past? There are lots of different answers to try. Luckily we're in a moment when many people are feeling newly activated against the police and for Black liberation. It is the perfect moment to start a renewed push to bring this movement about and see what a new generation has to say about these questions.

Epilogue

Veronica L.

I regret not contacting Butch sooner. She put her email address in her books. It wouldn't have been hard. But I felt intimidated and couldn't think of a good enough reason.

Her 2003 book, *The Military Strategy of Women and Children*, is the one I've read the most often. *Night-Vision* is a close second, but I've read all her stuff. Had a friend who passed me new ones as they came out, hoping I'd like them. I always did.

Befriending older marxist-leninists as a younger anarchist isn't something totally strange for me. I'm not the most ideological person, and I find older revolutionaries inspiring even if our political strategies and organizing cultures are different. Doubly so when it's someone who has never renounced the armed struggle tactics that were so much more prevalent in the long 60s. Triple if it's someone with interesting race and gender politics. And that was Butch.

Don't get me wrong, I knew we had differences. I asked her once if she was an anti-authoritarian, and she just said "well, what counts as authoritarianism?" It's a fair question, but also quite the dodge. Butch knew we had differences, too. She'd ask me why I was an anarchist when the anarchists seemed to have no strategy. My insurrectionary friends would say the lack of strategy is part of what makes us anarchists, but I didn't feel so sure. Despite that, Butch never tried to mould me into some sort of renegade maoist. She was unfailingly curious about my life and my political world and what I made of my own context, even if she did also really recommend that I read Lenin, which I still haven't done.

It feels weird to write about her so I'm hesitating a lot. There are many, many people who had more time with her than I did, who knew her better than I did, who I suspect aren't writing because that closeness with her means it maybe feels more like a betrayal to write about her. What do I even have to say really? I still have so many questions for her. There's so much she didn't tell me.

She wouldn't have wanted eulogizing so I'll try not to do it. But maybe it is particularly appropriate to share this here. Butch's response to Tammy is one of her most personal and autobiographical pieces of writing. It's also her last published work. I'm hoping, if she's anywhere watching me, she'll be okay with me reflecting publicly on what it meant to me to know her.

The first time I met her we hung out all day. I peppered her with questions and she tried to figure out my deal. She told me that the doctors said she had two years left to live. I wasn't sure whether to believe her or not, but she died almost two years to the day after we met.

We weren't in touch much in the first year. I didn't realize how bad she was at email. It took a global pandemic for me to pick up the phone and call her, and once I realized that was socially okay to do, I started calling her once a week. It was a weird time in everyone's lives, though I don't think the lockdown affected her much. By the time I met her, she already didn't leave the house often. On my end, the world was upside down and our weekly phone chats helped me feel to more connected to some sort of revolutionary community even if I was stuck at home.

At first, our phone calls were very business. Very "tell me the happs in your part of the world and why you think they're important/ what they mean and I'll tell you mine" kind of chats. In retrospect, maybe she was trying to teach me a way of analyzing the world around me so I could get clearer on what needs doing. Because she would never tell me what she thought I should do (beyond read certain things). She always said she didn't know what to do and the things she had tried didn't work and so it was up to my generation (and now the ones after me) to figure it out.

We talked about women's liberation a few times, and specifically the liberation of white women from white men in a move that might destroy whiteness once and for all. She told me that at one point, she tried to get her friends from the women-only dojo to all move into the same neighbourhood together but they wouldn't. She mentioned once that she regretted not joining a women's consciousness raising group. She was organizing with Appalachian women around welfare and housing issues instead.

When I wrote the response to her piece "On Reading Petronella Lee's Anti-fascism Against Machismo," she first told me that she didn't really like it but that she was gonna read it again and take it more seriously. I admit to having been confused. I thought I was stanning her. She wrote so much about white women leaving the table, I thought our ideas couldn't be far off. Then a friend said maybe Butch saw this kind of separatism as an ends not a means, and that seemed accurate. At one point in her life, Butch thought that the US would be broken up into separate nations and that perhaps one of those would be white women finally breaking free of white men.

In retrospect, one of the key differences between *The Military Strategy of Women and Children* and the "no cis-men"–style organizing of LIES is the military strategy. For all its prose and smart observations, LIES proposes no military strategy, and a big thing that disappointed Butch about the women's liberation movement was the lack of an army. Not just that, but the lack of the skills to even begin to think about how to organize an army for the liberation of women. So even if the liberation of white women from white men and gender abolition are related goals, Butch wanted a clearer strategic proposal that she wasn't getting from me or from LIES.

Another big difference is the way Butch wrote about gender as class. She told me on the phone once that she felt like she didn't understand the way people of my generation talk about gender. That the way we talk about gender made it more difficult for her to argue for gender as a class system. She's not wrong, and I'm still not entirely clear on the implications of it all and what that means for applying her theories today.

Butch tended to prioritize organizing with working-class people over organizing based on gender, and she worried the LIES proposal would make organizing spaces more homogenous. I assume a bunch of the actually existing feminist movement of her heyday would have felt alienating to her. She was a dyke who wasn't really a lesbian, a revolutionary who never renounced the guns, and a white woman who dreamed of geographic areas without white men but didn't think lesbian separatism was the way to get there.

Our phone calls were never very long. I did a lot of reading between the lines of what she was telling me. She, rightly, acted like the feds were listening to all our calls, and I knew better than to ask her more than she seemed comfortable sharing. She never asked me much about my life in specific, though I told her a bit about different projects I was working on, demos I would go to, etc. How much did we actually know about each other's lives? Very little. I'm sure she was filling in the gaps as much as I was between our conversations about demographics in LA, news about 1492 Land Back Lane, and what you could learn from riding the bus and talking to people.

In the fall of 2020, after six months of phone calls with Butch, I went to the countryside to help friends build a house, and Butch and I weren't in touch for a couple months. When I got back, something had happened, and I couldn't get her on the phone for another couple months. After that we would talk but she was more confused. Worried about me for reasons that I think weren't about me. Wanted to talk politics but struggled to keep up with the conversation. Some of our last calls involved her just saying "more more" as I tried to come up with interesting stories about political developments in the place where I live.

I called too late to say goodbye. But I'm also not sure she wouldn't have told me off if I'd tried to say goodbye. She didn't seem big on goodbyes.

If you knew Butch over the years and you wanna share reflections/thoughts with me, I'd so very appreciate it. In the spirit of leaving a contact email buried in the pages of a book, you can reach me at bottomfishbaby@proton.me or contact kersplebedeb and they know how to reach me.

Women's Antifascist Movement Conference
in the village of Čukorovac, Serbia, May 1944

Endnotes

Introduction

1. Daniel Paul, *We Were Not the Savages*, First Nations History, 4th ed. Fernwood Press, 2022.

2. Robert Devet, "How the Cornwallis Report Erases a History of Activism," *Nova Scotia Advocate* July 22, 2020. https://nsadvocate.org/2020/07/22/how-the-cornwallis-report-erases-a-history-of-activism/

3. Ibid.

4. Minister of National Defence Advisory Panel on Systemic Racism and Discrimination. *Final Report.* January, 2022. https://www.canada.ca/en/department-national-defence/corporate/reports-publications/mnd-advisory-panel-systemic-racism-discrimination-final-report-jan-2022.html

5. Robyn Bourgeois, "Let's call the Nova Scotia mass shooting what it is: White male terrorism," *The Conversation* April 24, 2020. https://theconversation.com/lets-call-the-nova-scotia-mass-shooting-what-it-is-white-male-terrorism-136938

Anti-Fascism Against Machismo:
Gender, Politics, and the Struggle Against Fascism

1. Ana Maria Tijoux, "We can't think of a feminism, an anti-patriarchy, without anti-capitalism," *Committee On U.S.-Latin American Relations*, March 8, 2017, https://cuslar.org/2017/03/10/ana-tijoux-we-cant-think-of-a-feminism-an-anti-patriarchy-without-anti-capitalism/

2. "How Anti-Fascists Won the Battles of Berkeley—2017 in the Bay and Beyond: A Play-by-Play Analysis," *CrimethInc.*, January 3, 2018, https://crimethinc.com/2018/01/03/how-anti-fascists-won-the-battles-of-berkeley-2017-in-the-bay-and-beyond-a-play-by-play-analysis.

3. Liz Fekete, "Anti-fascism or anti-extremism?" *Race & Class*, vol. 55, no. 4 (2014): 29–39.

4. Jason Wilson, "What do incels, fascists and terrorists have in common? Violent misogyny," *The Guardian*, May 4, 2018, https://www.theguardian.com/commentisfree/2018/may/04/what-do-incels-fascists-and-terrorists-have-in-common-violent-misogyny

5. Greg Wilford, "Heather Heyer: Charlottesville neo-Nazi rally organizer describes protester's death as 'payback'," *The Independent*, August 20, 2017, http://www.independent.co.uk/news/world/americas/jason- kessler- charlottesville-virginia-white-supremacist-rally-heather-heyer-payback-communist-a7903381.html

6. Maya Oppenheim, "GoDaddy Bans Neo-Nazi Site Daily Stormer for Defaming Charlottesville Victim Heather Heyer," *The Independent*, August 14, 2017, http://www.independent.co.uk/life-style/gadgets-and- tech/daily- stormer-godaddy-bans-charlotteville-victim-heather-heyer-victim-fat-slut-defame-uva-neo-nazi- a7891856.html

7. Cloee Cooper and Julia Taliesin, "White Nationalist Groups Turn Up At 2018 Women's Marches," *Political Research Associates*, February 2, 2018, https://politicalresearch.org/2018/02/02/white-nationalist-groups-turn-up-at-2018-womens-marches

8. Roy Batty, "Womyn Throw Protest on International Womyn's Day," *Daily Stormer*, 2018, https://dailystormer.name/womyn-throw-protest-on-international-womyns-day/

9. Maja Sager and Diana Mulinari, "Safety for whom? Exploring femonationalism and care-racism in Sweden," *Women's Studies International Forum*, vol. 68 (2018): 149–56.

10. "We Are Not Afraid: Chilean Feminism Rises in the Face of Fascist Attacks—Black Rose/Rosa Negra Statement on Opposing the Fascist Attacks and Stabbing of Three Feminist Activists in Chile," Black Rose Anarchist Federation, July 26, 2018, http://blackrosefed.org/we-are-not-afraid-chilean-feminism/

11. Joseph Luger, "Cultural Marxism is the #1 Enemy of Western Civilization," *Western Mastery*, March 23, 2017, http://www.westernmastery.com/2017/03/23/cultural-marxism-is-the-1-enemy-of-western-civilization/

12. Nicole Loroff, "Gender and Sexuality in Nazi Germany," *Constellations*, 3, no. 1 (2011): 49–61.

13. Matthew N. Lyons, "Ctrl-Alt-Delete: The origins and ideology of the Alternative Right," *Political Research Associates*, January 20, 2017, https://politicalresearch.org/2017/01/20/ctrl-alt-delete-report-on-the-alternative-right

14. Theodore Koulouris, "Online misogyny and the alternative right: debating the undebatable," *Feminist Media Studies*, 18, no. 4 (2018): 755.

15. Spencer Sunshine, "Three Pillars of the Alt-Right: White Nationalism, Antisemitism, and Misogyny," *Political Research*

Associates, December 4, 2017, https://politicalresearch.
org/2017/12/04/three-pillars-of-the-alt-right-white-nationalism-
antisemitism-and-misogyny

16. Matthew N. Lyons, "The alt-right hates women as much as
it hates people of colour," *The Guardian,* May 2, 2017, https://
www.theguardian.com/commentisfree/2017/may/02/
alt-right-hates-women-non-white-trump-christian-right-abortion

17. Aja Romano, "How the alt-right's sexism lures men into
white supremacy," *Vox,* April 26, 2018, https://www.vox.com/
culture/2016/12/14/13576192/alt-right-sexism-recruitment

18. Angela Nagle, *Kill All Normies: Online culture wars from 4chan and
Tumblr to Trump and the alt-right* (Alresford, UK: Zero Books, 2017).

19. Lyons, "Ctrl-Alt-Delete."

20. Matthew N. Lyons, "Alt-right: more misogynistic than many neo-
Nazis," *Three Way Fight,* December 3, 2016, http://threewayfight.
blogspot.com/2016/12/alt-right-more-misogynistic-than-many.
html

21. Romano, "How the alt-right's sexism lures men into white
supremacy."

22. Matt Lees, "What Gamergate should have taught us about the 'alt-
right,'" *The Guardian,* December 1, 2016, https://www.theguardian.
com/technology/2016/dec/01/gamergate-alt-right-hate-trump

23. Amelia Tait, "Spitting out the Red Pill: Former misogynists
reveal how they were radicalized online," *New Statesman,* February 28,
2017, https://www.newstatesman.com/long-reads/2017/02/
reddit-the-red-pill-interview-how-misogyny-spreads-online

24. Lyons, "Ctrl-Alt-Delete."

25. Nagle, *Kill All Normies,* 91.

26. Ibid, 88–89.

27. "The Rich Kids of Fascism: Why the Alt-Right Didn't Start with Trump, and Won't End With Him Either," *It's Going Down*, December 16, 2016, https://itsgoingdown.org/rich-kids-fascism-alt-right-didnt-start-trump-wont-end-either/

28. Alex DiBranco, "Mobilizing Misogyny," *Political Research Associates*, March 8, 2017, https://politicalresearch.org/2017/03/08/mobilizing-misogyny

29. Nagle, *Kill All Normies*, 92.

30. Ibid, 92–93.

31. Jeff Sparrow, "From misery to misogyny: incels and the far right," *Overland*, April 27, 2018, https://overland.org.au/2018/04/from-misery-to-misogyny-incels-and-the-far-right/

32. Zoe Williams, "'Raw hatred': why the 'incel' movement targets and terrorises women," *The Guardian*, April 25, 2018, https://www.theguardian.com/world/2018/apr/25/raw-hatred-why-incel-movement-targets-terrorises-women

33. Zack Beauchamp, "Incel, the misogynist ideology that inspired the deadly Toronto attack, explained," *Vox*, April 25, 2018, https://www.vox.com/world/2018/4/25/17277496/incel-toronto-attack-alek-minassian

34. Nellie Bowles, "Jordan Peterson, Custodian of the Patriarchy," *The New York Times*, May 18, 2018, https://www.nytimes.com/2018/05/18/style/jordan-peterson-12-rules-for-life.html

35. Bromma, "Exodus and Reconstruction: Working Class Women at the Heart of Globalization," *Kersplebedeb*, 2012, http://kersplebedeb.com/posts/exodus/

36. Hannah Gais, "The Alt-Right Doesn't Know What to Do With White Women," *The New Republic*, October 17, 2017, https://newrepublic.com/article/145325/alt-right-doesnt-know-white-women

37. Sunshine, "Three Pillars of the Alt Right."

38. Matthew N. Lyons, "Jack Donovan on men: a masculine tribalism far the far right," *Three Way Fight*, November 23, 2015, http://threewayfight.blogspot.com/2015/11/jack-donovan-on-men-masculine-tribalism.html

39. Anonymous, *The Unquiet Dead: Anarchism, Fascism, and Mythology* (2017), 11.

40. Shane Burley, *Fascism Today: What It Is And How To End It* (Chico: AK Press, 2017), 51.

41. Ibid, 91.

42. Matthew N. Lyons, "Notes on Women and Right-Wing Movements—Part One," *Three Way Fight*, September 27, 2005, http://threewayfight.blogspot.com/2005/09/notes-on-women-and-right-w_112787003380492443.html

43. Lyons, "Jack Donovan on men."

44. Jack Smith, "The women of the 'alt-right' are speaking out against misogyny. They'd prefer absolute patriarchy," *Mic*, December 8, 2017, https://www.mic.com/articles/186675/the-women-of-the-alt-right-are-speaking-out-against-misogyny-theyd-prefer-absolute-patriarchy

45. George Michael, "David Lane and the Fourteen Words," *Politics, Religion & Ideology*, vol. 10, no. 1 (2011): 43–61.

46. Kathleen M. Blee, "Women in the 1920s' Ku Klux Klan Movement," *Feminist Studies*, vol. 17, no. 1 (1991): 57–77.

47. Loroff, "Gender and Sexuality in Nazi Germany," 50.

48. Helen Zia, "White Power Women," *The Washington Post*, April 7, 1991, https://www.washingtonpost.com/archive/opinions/1991/04/07/white-power-women/a30050ed-cf61-46e2-a11f-3b2df977ea08/

49. "National Socialist Movement," *Southern Poverty Law Center*, no date, https://www.splcenter.org/fighting-hate/extremist-files/group/national-socialist-movement

50. "Mission Statement," *Women for Aryan Unity*, no date, archived at https://web.archive.org/web/20190305201827/http://www.wau14.com/mission-statement/. [The phrase "Race and Revolution" was later changed on the WAU website to "Folk and Revolution." See "About WAU," *Women for Aryan Unity*, no date, https://www.wau14.com/about/]

51. Dean Cornish, "Whining men: 'We're blamed for everything,'" *News.com.au*, July 4, 2018, https://www.news.com.au/lifestyle/real-life/true-stories/whining-men-were-blamed-for-everything/news-story/e2c27c0f6e5590e9f0373cd08cc09340

52. Proud Boys' Girls, *Twitter*, https://twitter.com/proudboysgirls.

53. David Futrelle, "'Gina tingles' and the Elders of Zion: Do Alt-Rightists hate women as much as they hate Jews?. *We Hunted The Mammoth*, June 14, 2017, https://www.wehuntedthemammoth.com/2017/06/14/gina-tingles-and-the-elders-of-zion-do-alt-rightists-hate-women-as-much-as-they-hate-jews/

54. Lyons, "Alt-right: more misogynistic than many neo-Nazis."

55. Gais, "The Alt-Right Doesn't Know What to Do With White Women."

56. Lyons, "Ctrl-Alt-Delete."

57. Donna Minkowitz, "Hiding in Plain Sight: An American Renaissance of White Nationalism," *Political Research Associates*, October 26, 2017, https://politicalresearch.org/2017/10/26/hiding-in-plain-sight-an-american-renaissance-of-white-nationalism

58. Sunshine, "Three Pillars of the Alt-Right."

59. Minkowitz, "Hiding in Plain Sight."

60. Chris Schiano, "Leaked: A Year Inside the Failed Neo-Nazi Traditionalist Worker Party," *Unicorn Riot*, April 5, 2018, https://www.unicornriot.ninja/2018/leaked-a-year-inside-the-failed-neo-nazi-traditionalist-worker-party/

61. A.C. Thompson, "Inside Atomwaffen As It Celebrates a Member for Allegedly Killing a Gay Jewish College Student," *ProPublica*, February 23, 2018, https://www.propublica.org/article/atomwaffen-division-inside-white-hate-group

62. James Kirchick, "A Thing for Men in Uniforms," *The New York Review of Books*, May 14, 2018, https://www.nybooks.com/online/2018/05/14/a-thing-for-men-in-uniforms/

63. Clay Bodnar, "Gay men and the Alternative Right: an overview," *Hope Not Hate*, April 11, 2018, https://hopenothate.org.uk/2018/04/11/gay-men-alternative-right-overview/

64. Johann Hari, "The Strange, Strange Story of the Gay Fascists," *Huffington Post*, October 21, 2008 (updated May 25, 2011), https://www.huffpost.com/entry/the-strange-strange-story_b_136697

65. Laurie Marhoefer, "Queer Fascism and the End of Gay History," *Notches*, June 19, 2018, https://notchesblog.com/2018/06/19/queer-fascism-and-the-end-of-gay-history/

66. Hari, "The Strange, Strange Story of the Gay Fascists."

67. Michael Abernethy, "Oxymorons: Gay Nazi, Gay Aryan, Gay Supremacist," *Pop Matters*, March 22, 2009, https://www.popmatters.com/72054-oxymorons-gay-nazi-gay-aryan-gay-supremacist-2496038330.html

68. Bodnar, "Gay men and the Alternative Right."

69. "New York's Alt Right (Part II)," *NYC Antifa*, December 6, 2016, https://nycantifa.wordpress.com/2016/12/06/new-yorks-alt-right-part-ii/

70. Donna Minkowitz, "How the Alt-Right Is Using Sex and Camp to Attract Gay Men to Fascism," *Slate*, June 5, 2017, https://slate.com/human-interest/2017/06/how-alt-right-leaders-jack-donovan-and-james-omeara-attract-gay-men-to-the-movement.html

71. Kirchick, "A Thing for Men in Uniforms."

72. James J. O'Meara, "The Rebirth of the *Männerbund* in Brian De Palma's *The Untouchables*," *Counter-Currents Publishing*, April 11, 2012, https://www.counter-currents.com/2012/04/brian-de-palmas-the-untouchables/

73. Lyons, "Jack Donovan on men."

74. Minkowitz, "How the Alt-Right Is Using Sex and Camp."

75. "The Wolves of Vinland: a Fascist Countercultural 'Tribe' in the Pacific Northwest," *Rose City Antifa*, November 7, 2016, https://rosecityantifa.org/articles/the-wolves-of-vinland-a-fascist-countercultural-tribe-in-the-pacific-northwest/

76. Nora Caplan-Bricker, "How a Bunch of Clowns Shut Down Anti-Migrant Vigilantes in Finland," *Slate*, February 1, 2016, https://slate.com/human-interest/2016/02/a-bunch-of-clowns-shut-down-anti-migrant-vigilantes-in-finland.html

77. Cindy Casares, "Trump's repeated use of the Mexican rapist trope is as old (and as racist) as colonialism," *NBC News*, April 7, 2018, https://www.nbcnews.com/think/opinion/trump-s-repeated-use-mexican-rapist-trope-old-racist-colonialism-ncna863451

78. Jamelle Bouie, "The Deadly History of 'They're Raping Our Women,'" *Slate*, June 18, 2015, https://slate.com/news-and-politics/2015/06/the-deadly-history-of-theyre-raping-our-women-racists-have-long-defended-their-worst-crimes-in-the-name-of-defending-white-womens-honor.html

79. Johannah May Black, "When Women Bear the Nation's Honour: Fascism and the Woman-as-Symbol Under Trump," *Revolutionary Anamnesis*, February 3, 2017, https://johannahmayblack. com/2017/02/03/when-women-bear-the-nations-honour-fascism-and-the-woman-as-symbol-under-trump/

80. Suvi Keskinen, "The 'crisis' of white hegemony, neonationalist femininities and antiracist feminism," *Women's Studies International Forum*, 68 (2018): 157–63.

81. Angela Davis, *Women, Race & Class* (New York: Random House, 1983), 107–108.

82. Ibid, 109.

83. Jackie Wang, "Against Innocence: Race, Gender, and the Politics of Safety," *LIES: A Journal of Materialist Feminism*, vol. 1 (2012): 164.

84. Andrea Smith, *Conquest: Sexual Violence and American Indian Genocide* (Durham: Duke University Press, 2005), 10.

85. Ibid, 23.

86. Joane Nagel, "Ethnicity and Sexuality," *Annual Review of Sociology*, vol. 26 (2000): 122.

87. Caitlin Carroll, "The European Refugee Crisis and the Myth of the Immigrant Rapist," *Europe Now Journal*, July 6, 2017, https:// www.printfriendly.com/p/g/wmsRa6

88. "Italian and Polish neo-nazis join forces to patrol beaches to 'protect women from migrants,'" *Freedom*, July 6, 2018, https:// freedomnews.org.uk/2018/07/06/italian-and-polish-neo-nazis-join-forces-to-patrol-beaches-to-protect-women-from-migrants/

89. Miriam Lafontaine, "La Meute Cancels Protest at Montreal Mosque Friday," *The Link*, December 14, 2017, https://thelinknewspaper.ca/article/la-meute-cancels-protest-at-montreal-mosque-friday

90. Minkowitz, "How the Alt-Right Is Using Sex and Camp."

91. Sally R. Munt "Gay shame in a geopolitical context," *Cultural Studies*, vol. 33, no. 2 (2019): 223–48.

92. Shon Faye, "We're Here, We're Queer, We're Racists," *Zed Books*, February 15, 2017, archived at https://web.archive.org/web/20210516031659/https://www.zedbooks.net/blog/posts/were-here-were-queer-were-racists/

93. Christine Hanhardt, *Safe Space: Gay Neighborhood History and the Politics of Violence* (Durham: Duke University Press, 2013), 223.

94. *The Unquiet Dead*, 7.

95. Isabelle Richet, "Women and Antifascism: Historiographical and Methodological Approaches," in *Rethinking Antifascism: History, Memory and Politics, 1922 to Present*, edited by Huge García, Mercedes Yusta, Xavier Tabet, and Cristina Clímaco (New York: Berghahn Books, 2016), 152–66.

96. Ingrid Strobl, *Partisanas: Women in the Armed Resistance to Fascism and German Occupation (1936–1945).* (Oakland: AK Press, 2008), xv.

97. Molly Crabapple, "Hidden Fighters: Remembering America's black antifascist vanguard," *The Baffler*, no. 35 (June 2017), https://thebaffler.com/salvos/hidden-fighters-crabapple.

98. Aregawi Berhe, "Revisiting resistance in Italian-occupied Ethiopia: The Patriots' Movement (1936–1941) and the redefinition of post-war Ethiopia," in *Rethinking Resistance: Revolt and Violence in African History*, edited by Jon Abbink, Mirjam de Bruijn, and Klaas van Walraven (Boston: Brill, 2003), 100.

99. Minale Adugna, *Women and Warfare in Ethiopia: A Case Study of Their Role During the Campaign of Adwa 1895/96, and the Italo-Ethiopian War, 1935–41*, Gender Issues Research Report Series, no. 13 (Organization for Social Science Research in Eastern and Southern Africa, 2001), 24.

100. Ibid, 31.

101. Ibid, 32.

102. Ibid, 2.

103. Ibid, 4.

104. Ibid, 26.

105. Ibid.

106. Denise Lynn, "Fascism and the Family: American Communist Women's Anti-fascism During the Ethiopian Invasion and Spanish Civil War," *American Communist History*, vol. 15, no. 2 (2016): 179.

107. Neelam Srivastava, "Anti-Colonialism and the Italian Left: Resistances to the Fascist Invasion of Ethiopia," *interventions*, vol. 8, no. 3 (2006): 427.

108. David Featherstone, "Black Internationalism, Subaltern Cosmopolitanism, and the Spatial Politics of Antifascism," *Annals of the Association of American Geographers*, vol. 103, no. 6 (2013): 1406–1420.

109. Crabapple, "Hidden Fighters."

110. Lisa Lines, *Milicianas: Women in Combat in the Spanish Civil War* (Lanham, MD: Lexington Books, 2015), 49.

111. Mary Nash, *Defying Male Civilization: Women in the Spanish Civil War* (Denver: Arden Press, 1995), 63.

112. Ibid, 78.

113. Martha Ackelsberg, *Free women of Spain: Anarchism and the struggle for the emancipation of women* (Bloomington: Indiana University Press, 1991), 115.

114. Ibid, 135.

115. Ibid, 147.

116. Chiara Bonfiglioli, "Women's Political and Social Activism in the Early Cold War Era: The Case of Yugoslavia," *Aspasia*, vol. 8 (2014): 1–25.

117. Jelena Batinic, "Gender, Revolution, and War: The Mobilization of Women in the Yugoslav Partisan Resistance During World War II" (Ph.D. dissertation, Department of History, Stanford University, 2009), 2.

118. Bonfiglioli, "Women's Political and Social Activism in the Early Cold War Era," 5.

119. Strobl, *Partisanas*, 53.

120. Ibid, 53–54.

121. Bonfiglioli, "Women's Political and Social Activism in the Early Cold War Era," 5.

122. Strobl, *Partisanas*, 54.

123. Batinic, "Gender, Revolution, and War," 126.

124. Strobl, *Partisanas*, 54.

125. Batinic, "Gender, Revolution, and War," 127.

126. Ibid, 126.

127. Ibid, 128.

128. Ibid, 97.

129. Ibid, 126.

130. Strobl, *Partisanas*, 55.

131. Batinic, "Gender, Revolution, and War," 130.

132. Rob Jackson, "There is No Such Thing as Revolutionary Inheritance," *Louise Michel Library Project*, February 12, 2019, https://louisemichellibraryproject.wordpress.com/2019/02/12/there-is-no-such-thing-as-revolutionary-inheritance/

133. Romina Akemi and Bree Busk, "Breaking the Waves: Challenging the Liberal Tendency within Anarchism," *Perspectives in Anarchist Theory*, June 29, 2016, https://anarchiststudies.org/breaking-the-waves-challenging-the-liberal-tendency-within-anarchist-feminism-by-romina-akemi-and-bree-busk/

134. Seattle Ultras, "Class Combat," *Ultra*, August 4, 2017, http://www.ultra-com.org/project/class-combat/

135. "On Ultras and Militant Structures," *It's Going Down*, April 22, 2017, https://itsgoingdown.org/on-ultras-and-militant-structures/

136. Sarah Jaffe, "The Long History of Antifa," interview with Mark Bray, *The Progressive*, September 13, 2017, https://progressive.org/latest/the-long-history-of-antifa-jaffe-170913/

137. Ashoka Jegroo, "Fighting Cops and the Klan: The History and Future of Black Antifascism," *Truthout*, February 21, 2017, https://truthout.org/articles/fighting-cops-and-the-klan-the-history-and-future-of-black-antifascism/

138. Editorial Committee, "Building Everyday Anti-Fascism," *Upping the Anti*, issue 19 (February 2, 2017), http://uppingtheanti.org/journal/article/19-building-everyday-anti-fascism/

139. Strobl, *Partisanas*.

On Reading Anti-Fascism Against Machismo

1. Max Fisher, "White Terrorism Shows 'Stunning' Parallels to Rise of Islamic State," *New York Times*, August 6, 2019.

2. Julie Bosman, Kate Taylor, and Tim Arango, "Many Gunmen in Mass Shootings Share a Hate Towards Women," *New York Times*, August 11, 2019.

3. Nicky Woolf, "Chilling Report details how Elliot Rodger executed murderous rampage," *The Guardian*, February 20, 2015; Peter Langman, PhD. *Transcript of Elliot Rodger's "retribution" Video*. https://schoolshooters.info/sites/default/files/rodger_video_1.0.pdf; "2014 Isla Vista killings – Wikipedia." https://en.wikipedia.org/wiki/2014_Isla_Vista_killings; Maya Rhodan, "Elliot Rodger: California Mass Shooter Had an Interest in Nazis," *Time*, February 19, 2015, https://time.com/3716041/elliot-rodger-california-mass-shooter-nazis-torture/.

4. Don Hamerquist, J. Sakai, Anti-Racist Action Chicago, Mark Salotte. *Confronting Fascism: Discussion Documents for a Militant Movement*. (Montreal and Chicago: Kersplebedeb, Arsenal & ARA Chicago, 2002), p. 74.

5. Robert B. Reich. *Aftershock* (New York: Knopf, 2010), p. 50.

6. Matthew S. Schwartz. "NASA Scrubs First All-Female Spacewalk For Want Of A Medium-Sized Suit," NPR.org, March 26, 2019.

Joining the Conversation

1. For those who don't know, #ShutDownCanada was a hashtag that came in the wake of yet another police raid on Wet'suwet'en territory in so-called British Columbia. Wet'suwet'en people have been blocking the path of a pipeline for more than a decade and in the past two years have faced two rounds of brutal raids and subsequent solidarity actions across the country. January 2020 was no different. In the wake of the raid, Kanien'kehá:ka people in so-called Ontario and Quebec blocked railroad tracks in solidarity with Wet'suwet'en people and the tactic spread widely. By the end of February there had been dozens of rail blockades, some lasting days, some lasting weeks.

2. Montréal Antifasciste. "Between National Populism and Neofascism: The State of the Far-Right in Québec in 2019." September 14, 2019. https://montreal-antifasciste.info/en/2019/09/14/between-national-populism-and-neofascism-the-state-of-the-far-right-in-quebec-in-2019/

3. Obviously there is a lot of overlap between the far-right and the uniformed police. However, most cities where these demonstrations are happening like to maintain at least the illusion that there is a separation and in some circumstances will penalize individual officers who are caught participating in far-right movements.

4. Here is a video of a white guy chasing and tackling another white guy who tried to break a window with the tweeter cheering it on https://twitter.com/queencitynerve/status/1266940913361850369?s=20.

5. Here is a video of a white guy breaking up paving stones with a hammer getting tackled and kicked by white guys, but handed over to the cops by what appears to be a mixed race group https://twitter.com/s_Allahverdi/status/1267240521052946432. Handing fellow demonstrators over to the police was a not-as-uncommon-as-it-should-be tactic used during the 2012 student strike by people who

became colloquially known as the paci-flics, a combination of the word pacifist and flic (cop).

6. Amber Hollibaugh, *My Dangerous Desires: A Queer Girl Dreaming Her Way Home.* Duke University Press 2000.

7. LIES II "To Make Many Lines, to Form Many Bonds," p. 59. They also point out that this practice of autonomy can also be used for other categories, for instance excluding white people.

8. Ibid., p. 58.

9. I'm taking it for granted here that autonomous organizing only makes sense when excluding categories of people who have access to power over other groups of people, so autonomous organizing that excludes cis people or white people makes total sense to me, while autonomous organizing that excludes trans people or people of colour makes no sense to me and, in fact, feels fashy. Didn't feel like this needed to be said cause it feels like common sense, but saying it here anyways. In this sentence specifically I'm also assuming that an autonomous space without men in my context would likely involve a lot of white women even if there were no (and shouldn't be any) intention to keep non-white non-men away from the project..

10. When I was finishing writing this text in the summer of 2020, #DisSonNom was taking off in Quebec. It started with a giant public call out of sexual violence in the "progressive community"; I did not know enough about it to sum it up correctly at the time, and I still feel that way in February 2023. There was a first demonstration that was huge, which included inspiring speeches and a brief shouting match with men in a Jeep holding a Trump flag. I felt hopeful and skeptical at the time and said so in the original footnote in this piece. In retrospect, the skeptical part of me was sadly proven right. From where I'm sitting, that demo was the peak of that struggle.

About the Authors

El Jones is a poet, journalist, educator and abolitionist living in Halifax, Nova Scotia. Her latest book, *Abolitionist Intimacies* (Fernwood Press) examines the movement to abolish prisons through Black feminist principles of love and mutual care. Her collection of spoken word, *Live from the Afrikan Resistance!* (Roseway Press) confronts white colonialism. She was the lead author of the report *Defunding the Police: Defining the Way Forward for HRM*. El is a co-founder of the Black Power Hour, a live Prison radio show on CKDU.

Tammy Kovich is a longtime anarchist based in Hamilton, Ontario. She loves dogs, hates patriarchy, and strives to be someone who puts her politics into practice on a daily basis. Her research interests include women's participation in riots, revolts, and revolutions; gender and anarchism; and contemporary feminist struggle.

Butch Lee (1940–2021) was an Amazon theorist. Her work deals with the need to understand women's struggles in both their class and military dimensions, as well as the fundamental importance of grasping the relationship between colonialism, neo-colonialism, and patriarchy. Her books include *The Military Strategy of Women and Children, Night-Vision: Illuminating War and Class on the Neo-Colonial Terrain*, and *Jailbreak Out of History: The Re-Biography of Harriet Tubman, & "The Evil of Female Loaferism."* Some of her other writings can be found at http://kersplebedeb.com/butchlee/

Veronica L. was raised in a white Catholic community in a super-segregated Rust Belt city in the usa. Her mom was active in the women's liberation movement in the 80s and raised her to be a feminist. It took moving away from home for her to find revolutionary anarchism, queer politics, and the surrounding subcultures that remain central to her life today. She lives in Montreal.

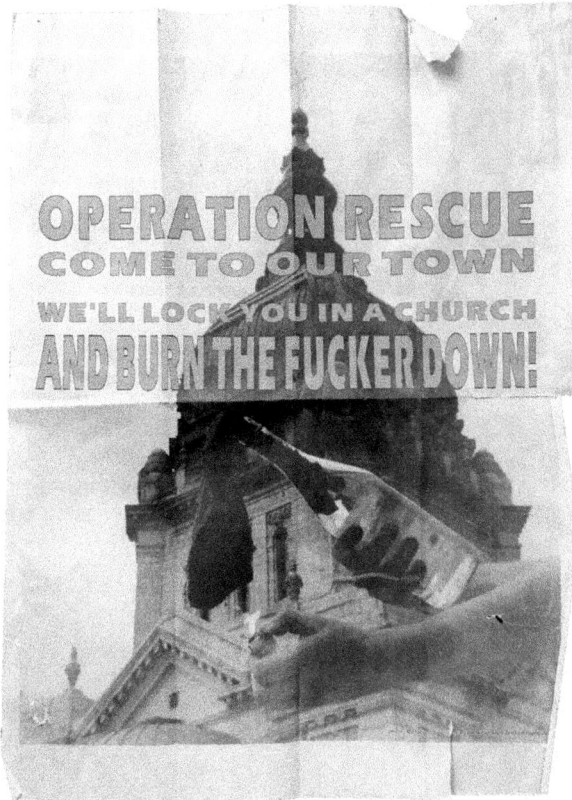

22 APRIL 1995

6 PM   AT THE RADISSON

777 UNIV.
CORNER
ST ANTOINE

METRO
SQUARE
VICTORIA

QUEER DEMO

It is vital to make the connection between women's rights, reproductive freedom, and lesbian and gay rights, for the fundamentalists surely do.

THEY OPENLY CALL FOR GAY BASHING.

THEY OPPOSE AIDS EDUCATION, SAFER SEX OR ANY KIND OF BIRTH- CONTROL.

In the words of HLI's founder and present-day chairman, Father Paul Marx:

"Does it annoy you when the media, the politicians and evem church leaders tell you homosexuals are 'just like everyone else'? Do you ever wish you had irrefutable scientific proof of how harmful homosexuality is? Your search is over. Let me send you The Gay Nineties by Paul Cameron." Cameron says "'I feel about homosexuality the way I feel about child molestation .... 'Even if carried out between consenting adults in their own homes, it is dangerous. It needs to be made illegal.'"

According to Father Alphonse de Valk, a longtime Canadian contact for HLI, **Absolutely Spine-chilling!**

"In religion, homosexual activity is an offense against God's law and, therefore a sin. In culture, lesbianism represents the asocial and totally repressive feminist rejection of men, while homosexuality is an abnormal preoccupation with self, leading to sexual egotism. Both result in the rejection of the family."

The Army Of God Speaks Out

"ALL ABORTION NURSES ARE LESBIANS. ABORTION GIVES THRILLS TO LESBIANS." Tom Metzger, fuhrer of white aryan resistance (War)

Butch, femme and androgynous dykes, leather queers, drag kings and queens, transsexuals and trans-genders Lesbian and gay people of color Lesbian and gay youth, people with AIDS and low-income QUEERS

WE HAVE TO RESPOND

WHEN WE FIGHT BACK TOGETHER, THEY DON'T

HAVE A PRAYER!

Fighting abortion is just a front for Human Life International; what the U.S.-based group really wants is to create a white Christian heterosexual world

TIME TO FIGHT BACK Against Bigots BE A QUEER FOR CHOICE! PROTEST AGAINST HLI

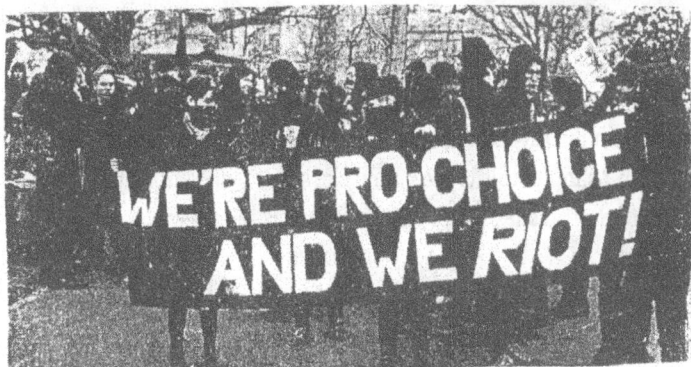

July 5-19 Operation "Rescue"

anti-abortion fanatics are traveling through California this summer attacking women, our clinics, and our healthcare providers. They are coming to San Jose, San Francisco, and the East Bay and on up to Redding and Sacramento.

BE PART OF THE PRO-CHOICE RESISTANCE TO THE HOLY TERRORISTS !

Get out to defend the clinics, July 5th - July 19th at 5:30 am.

San Francisco: Pregnancy Consultation Center, 1801 Bush @ Octavia. **East Bay:** Pregnancy Consultation Center, 400 40th St.,@ Shatter, Oakland. **San Jose:** Women's Community Clinic, 696 E. Santa Clara @ 13th.

You are especially needed July 9th, 10th, & 11th when O.R. will be in the San Jose and San Francisco areas.

Come demonstrate and expose Operation "Rescue" at their recruitement rallys:

In Danville: July 9, 6:30 pm. Rolling Hills Community Church, 1565 Green Valley Road, Danville. Car pools leave Ashby Bart at 5 pm.

In Sacramento: July 16, 6:30 pm. Crossroads Christian Fellowship, 5501 Dewey, Sacramento. Car pools leave Ashby Bart at 4:30 pm.

Get trained in Clinic Defense:

- Thursday, June 30th: San Francisco, PCC, 1801 Bush @ Octavia, 6:30 pm.
- Saturday, July 2nd: San Francisco, PCC, 1801 Bush @ Octavia, noon
- Thursday, July 7th: Berkeley, Martin Luther King Jr. Park, MLK @ Center 6:30 pm.

For More Information:
In S.F: BACORR NORTH

or CARAL
In San Jose: BACORR SOUTH

In Sac: SACORR .

Three Way Fight:
an insurgent blog on the struggle against the state and fascism

Three Way Fight is a blog that promotes revolutionary antifascist analysis, strategy, and organizing. Unlike liberal antifascists, we believe that "defending democracy" is an illusion, as long as that "democracy" is based on a socio-economic system that exploits and oppresses human beings. At the same time, unlike many on the revolutionary left, we believe that fascists and other far rightists aren't simply tools of the ruling class, but represent an autonomous political force that clashes with capitalist interests in real ways.

Radicals need to confront both the established capitalist order and an insurgent or even revolutionary right, while recognizing that these opponents are also in conflict with each other. Our blog confronts complexities in the dynamics between these three poles that are often glossed over. We point out, for example, that repression isn't necessarily fascist—antifascism itself can be a tool of ruling-class repression (as was the case during World War II, when anti-fascism was used to justify strike-breaking and the mass imprisonment of Japanese Americans, among other measures). And we warn against far right efforts to build alliances with leftists as well as fascistic tendencies within the left (as when leftists promote conspiracy theories rooted in anti-Jewish scapegoating).

Three Way Fight was initiated in 2004 as a collaborative project by several radical antifascist organizers. From the beginning, Three Way Fight has brought together anarchist and independent Marxist perspectives, and has sought to promote inclusive discussion and debate among revolutionary leftists. Our work is intended as a contribution to larger conversations among all those who are committed to liberatory change.

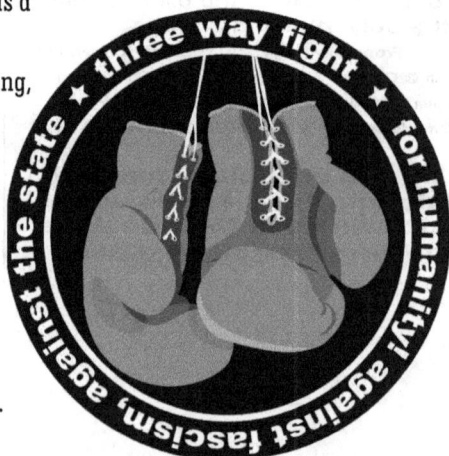

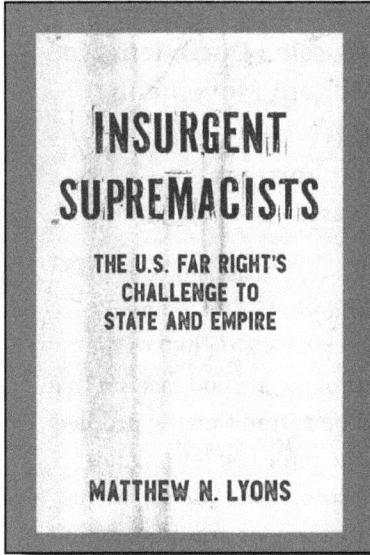

Insurgent Supremacists: The U.S. Far Right's Challenge to State and Empire

MATTHEW N. LYONS

9781629635118 • 384 PAGES $24.95

A major study of movements that strive to overthrow the U.S. government, that often claim to be anti-imperialist and sometimes even anti-capitalist yet also consciously promote inequality, hierarchy, and domination, generally along explicitly racist, sexist, and homophobic lines. Revolutionaries of the far right: insurgent supremacists. In this survey of enemy terrain, Matthew N. Lyons takes readers on a tour of neonazis and Christian theocrats, by way of the patriot movement, the LaRouchites, and the alt-right. Supplementing this, thematic sections explore specific dimensions of far-right politics, regarding gender, decentralism, and anti-imperialism.

Intervening directly in debates within left and antifascist movements, Lyons examines both the widespread use and abuse of the term "fascism," and the relationship between federal security forces and the paramilitary right. His final chapter, written in 2017, offers a preliminary analysis of the Trump presidential administration relationship with far-right politics and the organized far right's shifting responses to it.

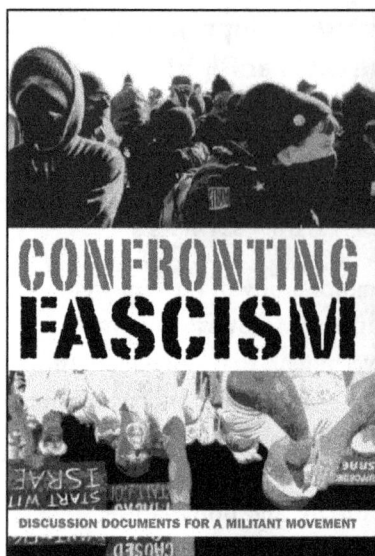

Confronting Fascism: Discussion Documents for a Militant Movement

DON HAMERQUIST, J. SAKAI,

MARK SALOTTE, XTN

978-1-894946-87-2 • 219 PAGES $14.95

In his text "Fascism & Antifascism" Don Hamerquist takes a wrecking ball to the mythology around fascism that had been traditionally peddled by the reformist left. Against objections that fascists are just a distraction, or are simple-minded agents of the state and capital, he shows how fascism contains a revolutionary and even anticapitalist impulse thoroughly enmeshed with its own deeply oppressive and anti-liberatory politics. Unraveling what this means for antifascists and our strategies is the task at hand, and Hamerquist proceeds to lay down some important preliminary realities that we need to deal with.

J. Sakai follows Hamerquist, interrogating his analysis as he pushes it forward. Sakai argues against the idea that fascism comes primarily from the working class, just as he extends the point that fascism is not an inherently or essentially "white" ideology. A discussion of different forms of capitalist rule, the class structure of global imperialism, and the history of anticapitalist critique within both Italian and German "classical" fascism, flows into a contemporary contextualization of fascism within the neocolonial context.

Shorter texts from the *ARA Research Bulletin*, Mark Salotte, and Xtn of ARA Chicago, place these theoretical insights in the concrete context of the political and physical fight against the far right, while also recovering the connections between this fight and the broader rise of anticapitalist struggle at the time.

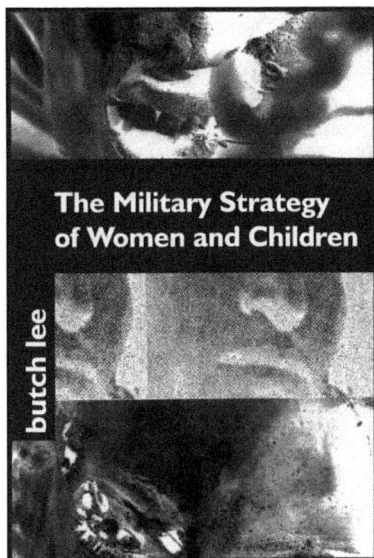

The Military Strategy of Women and Children

BUTCH LEE • 0973143231

116 PAGES • $12.00

Lays out the need for an autonomous and independent women's revolutionary movement, a revolutionary women's culture that involves not only separating oneself from patriarchal imperialism, but also confronting, opposing, and waging war against it by all means necessary.

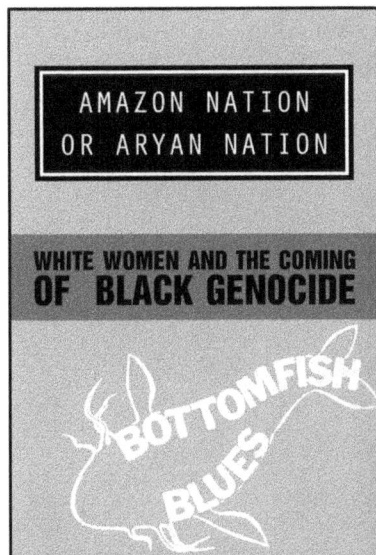

Amazon Nation or Aryan Nation: White Women and the Coming of Black Genocide

BOTTOMFISH BLUES • 9781894946551

168 PAGES • $12.95

The two main essays in this book come from the radical women's newspaper Bottomfish Blues, which was published in the late 1980s and early 90s; while a historical appendix on "The Ideas of Black Genocide in the Amerikkkan Mind" was written more recently, but only circulated privately. These texts provide raw and vital lessons at the violent crash scene of nation, gender, and class, from a revolutionary perspective.

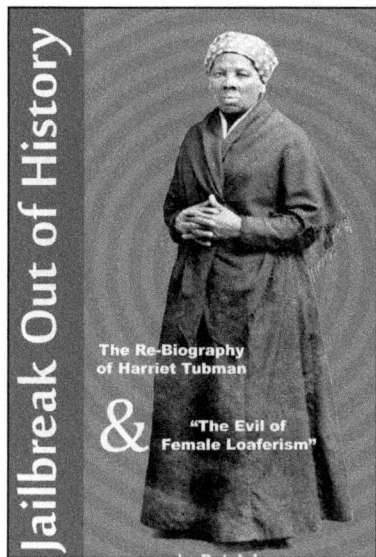

Jailbreak Out of History: the Re-Biography of Harriet Tubman & "The Evil of Female Loaferism", 2nd edition

BUTCH LEE

9781894946704 • 169 PAGES • $14.95

In *Jailbreak Out of History*, revolutionary Amazon theorist Butch Lee shows how the anticolonial struggles of New Afrikan/Black women were central to the unfolding of 19th century amerika, both during and "after" slavery.

The book's title essay, "The Re-Biography of Harriet Tubman," recounts the life and politics of Harriet Tubman, who waged and eventually led the war against the capitalist slave system. As Lee explains, "Harriet Tubman was a radical political figure, someone totally involved as a player in the great political ideas and military storms of her day. She was a guerrilla. Someone who lived and taught others to live by the communal and working-class New Afrikan culture that her people had planted in this difficult ground, and a Black Feminist to the end."

Jailbreak Out of History's second essay, written in 2014, picks up the story where "Re-Biography" leaves off, showing how New Afrikan women's labor and resistance remained central to how the global class struggle played out in the united states after the white men's Civil War came to an end.

KER
SPL
EBE
DEB

Since 1998 Kersplebedeb has been an important source of radical literature and agit prop materials.

The project has a non-exclusive focus on anti-patriarchal and anti-imperialist politics, framed within an anticapitalist perspective. A special priority is given to writings regarding armed struggle in the metropole, the continuing struggles of political prisoners and prisoners of war, and the political economy of imperialism.

The Kersplebedeb website presents historical and contemporary writings by revolutionary thinkers from the anarchist and communist traditions.

Kersplebedeb can be contacted at:

Kersplebedeb
CP 63560
CCCP Van Horne
Montreal, Quebec
Canada
H3W 3H8

email: info@kersplebedeb.com
web: www.kersplebedeb.com
www.leftwingbooks.net

Kersplebedeb

www.ingramcontent.com/pod-product-compliance
Lightning Source LLC
Chambersburg PA
CBHW060458280326
41933CB00014B/2783